BEYOND THE GODS

Facing life's biggest questions, like the meaning of existence, without any supernatural support

Praise for *Beyond the Gods*

"With the implacable rigorousness known to those of us who have read his books and articles on film and on travel, Nicholas E. Meyer here delves into riskier territory, the frameworks of fantasy and violence on which civilization has rested: religion. Freud had foreseen *The Future of an Illusion*; nearly a century later, it has been shown that the illusion in question was much more enduring than the Viennese sage had assumed. In *Beyond the Gods*, Meyer takes apart (or, in current usage, "deconstructs") the various mechanisms that led to the setting up of cults and doctrines, the fallacies that were imposed on us (with a reversal of the burden of proof: it is we who end up having to prove they were false), in a millennia-long story that led millions of people to become, in the best of cases, submissive individuals, and in the worst, the victims of religious fanaticism.

"Meyer's style is clear and straightforward: although the book shows a solid grounding and sources, it's in no way solely geared to readers who are especially erudite or trained in the sometimes abstruse verbal pirouettes of philosophy.

"*Beyond the Gods* is a book for everyone, and especially for those who, still hiding in the closet of atheism, will herein find the keys to at last come out of it—emerging guilt-free."

Marcelo Zapata, novelist (*Puccini's Secret*) and playwright (*Brutus*).

"Why did this initially remind me of a novel, although *Beyond the Gods* isn't fiction, but sheer philosophy and even theology? Because Nicholas E. Meyer's vein as an author of fiction (*An Irish Shade in Patagonia*, unpublished) shines through, which makes reading the book much more congenial for those of us who aren't career philosophers. His facet as an illustrator also emerges when he draws amusing, eloquent and even didactic creatures, in a very individual style.

"This thinking machine that is N.E.M. is capable of injecting real drollery into the unfolding rigorousness of his arguments. As I read him I was reminded of John Updike's *Roger's Version* in which a student with a contrarian sense of humor accumulates irrefutable words about the existence of God.

"I end the joyous philosophical-theological journey, offered by this truthful, very contemporary and unique writer, fuelled up and with some answers for my life as a female Christian atheist."

Marta Nos, prizewinning novelist (*The Laborious Path of the Water*) and short-story writer (*Kill, Jocasta, Kill*).

"In grappling with the meaning of life, we all too often opt for faith in a supernatural power as the safest choice. In this lively and penetrating book, Nicholas E. Meyer dismantles the belief that a god or gods have the first and last word on our existence.

"Meyer's simple tool is reason, applied methodically.

"The dark side of faith as a font of intolerance and violence is self-evident, but this book goes further, demonstrating how all the rituals and rules of religions fail the test of reason. To the question of the meaning of life, *Beyond the Gods* offers an answer."

Alan Riding, author (*Distant Neighbours: A Portrait of the Mexicans*; books on French culture, Shakespeare and opera) and playwright (*Liberators*).

BEYOND THE GODS

Facing life's biggest questions, like the meaning of existence, without any supernatural support

Nicholas E. Meyer

HYPATIA PRESS

Published by Hypatia Press in the United Kingdom in 2025

ISBN: 978-1-83919-677-5

Illustrations by Nicholas E. Meyer

www.hypatiapress.org

To my grandsons, Lucas and Tommy.

And in memory of Gustavo Ponce de León and Carlos Gamir Sampere.

CONTENTS

PART I: WHY?

CHAPTER 1
GOALS

This book doesn't seek to convince anybody to either believe or disbelieve (or do or not do) anything.

Instead it provides a way forward for people who have already dropped all supernatural beliefs—but experience a nagging feeling that they are at fault, in the following way.

Faced with what can loosely be termed the "Big Questions" in life—the really big ones, like the very meaning of life, the origin of the world, the afterlife, and so on—they have rejected the answers traditionally provided by religion. They have found those "answers" to be irrational and false: not answers at all. However, they may think that perhaps they should be replacing them with others, or facing them in a different manner, and haven't had time to come up with much.

They may have got as far as deciding that it would be pointless to just replace one set of pseudo-answers with others that are equally untenable. And—crucially—they refuse the easy, or cowardly, way out of simply trying to avoid thinking about these matters.

Quite the contrary: they consider that it should at least be possible to develop an *approach* to the Big Questions in life that doesn't duck the issues—yet remains firmly agnostic (this book agrees that this should be possible). But they haven't got around to developing such an approach. This book does.

If agnostic-minded people don't, on their own, think that something needs to be done about the Big Questions, the believers among their friends—if they talk about these things—will soon enough tell them so.

"How can you *live* if you don't believe in anything?" "If God didn't create the world, who did?" "If people didn't believe in God, what would keep them from killing and stealing and other dreadful things?" "Wouldn't life be completely pointless if we didn't have a soul that lives on after we die?" And so on. If you are one of the disbelievers, you will probably have heard all of these examples and more. You yourself may have posed them— to yourself.

Except that, unlike your theistic friends, you haven't taken the existence of these queries as proof, in itself, that you need to fall back on religion, or on superstition or on any other beliefs in otherworldly beings or forces.

But the nagging feeling may persist.

You may have pointed to yourself as living proof that it is indeed perfectly possible to live without the support of religious beliefs.

Your friends argue that total disbelief is impossible. The fact that you are able to produce a living, breathing counter-example to this—namely yourself—should in principle strike them as a strong argument, at least from the standpoint of strict logic. If they go for strict logic. And as long, of course, as they know you to be conscientious, thoughtful, demonstrably unparalyzed by any fear of oblivion after death, and humane, or at least uncriminal—and all of this without any god or gods to compel, hector, or comfort you. It would be pointless to present yourself as an example that life can be lived without the backing and guidance of gods, if they are convinced that you are irredeemably shallow, cruel, and a hopeless dimwit. (Perhaps it's best not to put them to this particular test—it may not be wise to delve too deeply into what our friends think of us, insofar as they do so at all).

I hardly need to add that logical arguments anyway cannot make a real dent in their religious belief if it is authentically such, religion being based on faith, not reason, as religious people usually (not always) emphasize. At best they will mutter that your claim to an utter lack of supernatural beliefs can't be true—that there must be something, some fears, some secret plea for rock-solid answers to the Big Questions, that you are hiding from them or even from yourself.

At worst, they will—even if they politely decline to mention it—sadly reach the conclusion that you are, after all, not only misguided but, despite appearances, probably evil too. As a minimum, amoral.

At any rate, they won't be convinced by your argument. But it is *your* state of mind that really interests us here, not theirs. You may still think there should also be some more detailed and specific rejoinders to the theistic prodding or heckling, and in fact to the Big Questions themselves. That's the nagging feeling referred to at the beginning.

And you're right. Some powerful responses *are* possible. The chapters that follow spell out a full set. Let it be again underlined that they do not replace religion's answers with another set of answers that are equally anchored in nothing but faith or an ability to provide psychological reassurance.

There's a fundamental fact that one needs to be aware of. The Big Questions divide into two groups. Some, including some of the biggest—like "what is the meaning of life?" or "does the soul exist?"—can be answered outright, fully disposed of, and will be in these pages. Those in the other group turn out, on examination, to be unanswerable (in principle, or just in our current state of knowledge); and for this other group, the valid—meaning non-otherworldly—way to broach them is also different. It is to take a major step that religion, of course, doesn't take, which is to realize that it's better to *recognize* them as unanswerable, and adjust to this fact, than to paper them over with "answers" that aren't. For avoiding what is not of this world, that is the approach.

There is a second group of persons for whom this book is written, namely those who are hesitant on the matter. They would like to abandon religion because they see it as unjustified, and in fact in their daily lives handle themselves entirely without recourse or reference to any god or gods. But they haven't let go entirely, because they'd like to have a better idea of how the Big Questions could then be faced.

Lastly, these pages are also intended for people who haven't given these issues much thought at all; who are content to have their lives unfold against the backdrop of the answers handed down by religion; but who, if they discover that a different approach actually exists—a sturdily secular-minded one—might find it much better attuned to their needs, both intellectual and emotional.

Nevertheless, it should be stressed over and over that this is not a book that's primarily concerned with presenting arguments against religion, or against otherworldly beliefs in general. It will necessarily become involved with some essential ideas on the matter. In fact, the initial part of what follows marshals a line of reasoning about the falsehood of such beliefs—and then about their dangerousness (at least three distinct types of danger). But that is simply because, once it is done in this way, what needs to be said about each specific Big Question is actually quite brief—it all just clicks into place. There are a number of good books in existence devoted specifically to presenting the case against the gods.

What this text is, instead, is a *complement* to that kind of book: this is a kind of how-to guide to coping with the key puzzles that have accompanied mankind for millennia, *after* the departure of the deities that were seen as the answer for virtually all of that time.

The basic approach developed here isn't rocket science. Anybody could come up with it. However, doing so requires an investment in time spent thinking about it, and even more for dealing methodically, one after the other, with each Big Question and each secondary query. Most people are, naturally, too busy getting on with their lives to invest that time.

Incidentally, some of the commonsense arguments employed here may look so simple as to seem naive alongside the wonderful subtlety of some religious disputation. They do have an unbeatable advantage, though. They work.

And to possess a philosophy for comprehensively dealing with life without recourse to the supernatural, nothing more complex, or longer, is needed than what is contained here.

So, for some of us at least—though certainly not for most of the rest of the globe—the gods have said their good-byes, and have left the stage.

With regard to life's Big Questions, what now?

CHAPTER 2
IRRATIONALISM, SUPERSTITION, SECTS, AND RELIGIONS

If two people or groups of people have been arguing over a difference in beliefs, that difference will loom very large to them, because they are close to it. But it will seem small to someone who has a completely separate set of beliefs from those of either. Example: the difference between Catholic and Protestant, or between Christian and Muslim, is huge for those people, in any of those groups, who care deeply about the issue. Yet, for those who aren't monotheists at all—say, Hindus—the difference appears minor compared to the chasm between all of them, lumped together as monotheistic religions, and the knowledge, obvious to them, that the world is *full* of deities.

This is no more than a consequence of the fact that things, or the distances between things, look bigger when you are up close than when you are afar. We consider ourselves to be distant from Pluto, but for someone looking at both us and Pluto from a faraway star, the distance between us is hardly detectable.

And that's not a moral judgment on the faraway observer's part; it's optics.

What is this leading up to? For a person who really "doesn't believe in anything," in the sense that believers use the phrase, there isn't all that much of a difference (except as regards whether they tend to be physically threatening or not) between various trends within a given religion, between different religions, between monotheistic and polytheistic religions, between established religions and sects, between those that to outsiders at least seem sincere and those that don't, or between any of the above and beliefs in things like telekinesis, fortune-telling, magic, astrology, omens and so on.

It's certainly not that non-believers don't perceive the differences, both subtle and large, between all those positions; they do. It's just that there's one thing that all those positions share: they're ultimately not rational, but faith-based, whether the faith is in supernatural beings or in supernatural phenomena. (What's so great about having a rational grounding, since rationality is open to a variety of criticisms? The issue is acknowledged here, but will be dealt with more conveniently later in the book.) And the difference between the rational and the non-rational is greater than between *varieties* of non-rational belief.

The above may offend various believers: it's not intended to. But notice two things:

First, it is not a moral judgment; it's "optics," i.e. merely a consequence of standing at a greater remove. Second, even unintended offense may work in two different directions. Traditionally religious people may feel insulted by having their stately and time-honored practices and beliefs tossed together with sects, which they may regard as the realm of charlatans, or with mere superstitions, which they may consider beneath contempt. Yet on the other hand, people who are convinced, for example, that yellow is an unlucky color, but who otherwise "believe in nothing," may be indignant at being lumped together with religious people whom they see as burdened by absurdly complex structures of beliefs, taboos, prayers and prescribed activities. Further, they may point out that believers solely in unlucky colors have never burned disbelievers at the stake.

CHAPTER 3
CUTTING THROUGH AMBIGUITY

I have been using the word "belief." It's important to try to approximate what I mean by that, or else I could get caught by the following kind of prankster (many non-believers will have come across him or her).

Prankster: Oh, so you claim you don't "believe in anything." By the way, what time is it?

Me: I don't have a watch on me, but I believe it's around four o'clock.

Prankster: Ah, so you do believe in something!

Ha, ha.

Obviously, the word "belief" has many different meanings, and the prankster has illegitimately jumped from one to another. The language (any spoken, non-logical language, and English more so than some others) is steeped in ambiguity and polysemy—diversity of meanings. That's what makes language so rich, so much fun, and for some purposes so frustrating.

To illustrate just how many meanings the idea of "belief" can have, in each of the following sentences the phrase "I believe" is used in a different way, though sometimes the difference is just a fine nuance (and then again, fine nuances can lead to serious dis-agreements, as any contract lawyer knows):

"I believe tomorrow the Earth will continue to rotate on its axis."

"I believe tomorrow it will rain."

"I believe the capital of France is Paris."

"I believe the capital of Swaziland is either Mbabane or Ma-seru."

"I believe in democracy."

"I believe in the human capacity for goodness."

"I believe Max will return the $100 I lent him."

"I believe I did the right thing in lending him the money."

"I believe God created the universe."

"I believe someone put a hex on me."

And there are surely other meanings. "When I make a word do a lot of work like that," says Humpty Dumpty in *Through the Looking-Glass and What Alice Found There*, "I always pay it extra." If these fair-employment practices of Humpty Dumpty's were in-deed applied to "believe," it would be a wealthy word.

So at this point I'll tell you one thing I do believe: I believe it's a waste of time to play wordgames, when what we're trying to do is get on with establishing rational approaches to life's Big Questions. Further, I believe that what is necessary in order to achieve that aim is not to provide a perfectly watertight and exactly inclu-sive definition, which nobody has ever done, but to have the reader understand what is meant in each circumstance.

How is understanding achieved despite all the nuances and polysemy in the language? It's easy in practice, actually. All of us do it all the time: we catch the sense of a word from context and experience (and, in spoken conversation, also from inflection and gesture). And we move on.

Groping for very exact definitions of some of the key words used here is even less essential than usual for texts that employ them. A book by a religious person who wants to anathematize sects, for example, may need to be very careful in establishing the boundary between a religion and a sect. But for someone standing at such a distance from either that the boundaries cease to matter much—well, they matter less.

In sum: this book uses "believe" in the usual sense in which it's used by believers themselves, as exemplified in such sentences as "John believes in God," "Jennifer doesn't believe in ghosts," and "Roderick believes a rabbit's foot brings good luck." (Roderick being impervious to the thought that the unfortunate rabbit had four, and look how it ended up.)

CHAPTER 4
IS ATHEISM A BELIEF?

While on the subject of the use of the word "belief," there is an issue to be dealt with, the idea that atheism is, at heart, also a belief. Making this claim appears to give the believers some psychological satisfaction.

"I believe God exists," they'll say. "You believe God doesn't exist. What's the difference? They are both beliefs. So *there!*"

But there *is* a difference—in logic.

Suppose I tell you the world is crammed with invisible beings constantly in motion and constantly changing in shape, who are right-handed one day and left-handed the next, and cross in the mornings and pleased in the afternoons, and very learned on Mondays and Thursdays and ignoramuses the rest of the week. More than that: they have a clear genealogy—who begat whom—except during leap years, when they are all simply brothers and sisters. These beings, I further tell you, are called ytreqs, and although quite impossible to detect in any way, actually closely control our destiny. They never create anything, but are in charge of the fate of everything once it has been created; most of the time, they take delight in destroying things, except when they feel itchy, because on those occasions they are extremely merciful. They can be prayed to, but during election periods they prefer outright bribes—did I mention they hold elections? Unless it rains, in which case they establish dictatorships.

You will tell me (I hope!) that you don't believe in ytreqs. (Not that ytreqs are a lot more absurd than some of the things that many people manage to believe without batting an eyelid. It's just that, being new, their absurdity is manifest, as it lacks the camouflage that familiarity confers on other outlandish beliefs). And you will point out—quite rightly—that your disbelief, or "belief in their non-existence," is not of the same kind as my belief in them, because you are not required to prove to me that ytreqs don't exist. *It is I who must prove that they do.*

This asymmetrical nature of the need to provide proof, when faced with someone of the opposite persuasion, is what makes belief in existence and belief in non-existence different things.

Believers may have no need to offer proof of their beliefs to themselves, or to other believers, if they are satisfied that it's a question of faith, not proof. But if they take it upon themselves to argue with non-believers, they have to prove the existence of what they believe in. The disbelievers have no need to prove anything.

Individually, they may choose to even make it their life's work to argue against religion or refute arguments in favor of the existence of gods (or enchantments or the transmigration of the soul or the evil eye or whatever). They may do so for such reasons as hoping to free people from mental shackles. But there's no obligation.

Belief and disbelief are (at least logically, and thus for people who are prepared to accept logic) two different things—not mirror images.

There is also a more compressed refutation to the claim that non-belief is also a belief. Just say: "I believe that God doesn't exist, in the same way, and to the same extent, that I believe that fairies don't exist, that unicorns don't exist, and that Godzilla doesn't exist."

CHAPTER 5
AT THE ROOT OF RELIGIOUS BELIEF

Why were the Big Questions posed in the first place? Religious feeling (in the widest sense, i.e., including even what most people would agree are isolated superstitions) is the product of psychological drives which are not only multiple but even contradictory. To consider that such a complex human phenomenon as religiosity responds to just one kind of primordial impulse, or is meant to satisfy just one need, would necessarily cloud our understanding.

Thus mankind has endowed its gods and its religions with a wealth of features that meet a whole range of needs. One very strong drive among humans, for example, is the impulse to follow a strong leader, and even to abase themselves before him—rarely her. Or, at least, to clearly indicate their submission to him; there are biological bases for this. But at the same time, humans tend to feel grandly self-important, at the apex of creation, in command of nature (much of the time, anyway), and so on. Yet even then, they have constant cause to remember their shortcomings.

For all these situations, gods are a great comfort. Gods are something to cower before, to feel insignificant in relation to, to worship, to abase oneself before, to try to cuddle up to.

Simultaneously, though—here's the beauty of it—gods aggrandize us, because they are so like us, only more so. Humans acutely feel the limitations of their power, so their gods are powerful—in some cases, all-powerful. Humans gnash their teeth at their mortality, so their gods are immortal. Everything we can only wish we had, our gods can have; it's the most wonderful psychological compensation device possible, because to some extent, we can identify with our gods, since they tend to be anthropomorphic. In the Jewish tradition and those that are derived from it, God specifically creates man in his own image. (Which is only natural. As Montesquieu noted, "If triangles had a god, he would have three sides.")

These effects are clearly contradictory. On one hand the gods drive home to us how minuscule, how contingent we are, while on the other, the gods jack up our self-esteem because they are essentially ourselves, with desirable super-features added. But the contradiction doesn't faze believers for an instant, for the human mind is awesome in its power to absorb contradictions; it positively thrives on antinomies.

Historically, people have often discovered that they could take their assumptions about the nature and properties of their gods—and carefully reason themselves into a tangle. Time and again, rather than force themselves to settle for one or the other among opposing conclusions—much less question their original assumptions—they have preferred to play it safe and cover all bases, i.e., accept and digest the paradoxes whole.

This is called achieving a mystical fusion of the opposites, or some similar wording. And with that, the impossible is accepted.

"Mystical" means leaving it fuzzy. One just lets oneself go with the pleasing, heart-filling feel of it.

A good example of ideas that a religion may happily retain even after they are shown to be paradoxical is the godly attribute of omnipotence. (It isn't essential; the Greek gods weren't omnipotent. Even Zeus, their *capo di tutti capi*, had to keep watching his back when going about his habitual philandering, because of his jealous wife Hera.) Omnipotence can be demolished, as an idea, by the old gag used by naughty children to taunt their catechism teachers, "If God is omnipotent, can he make a stone so heavy that he himself can't lift it?" A possible reaction to the discovery that the attribute leads to logical contradiction *might* have been to say something like, "Well, it was just a pleasing idea. Let's try something else." Needless to say, that's not what happened. In matters of belief, the human mind seems to find it easier to accept this kind of logical nonsense than to backtrack with regard to an assumption, once adopted.

Can God create a logical enigma so complex that even he can't solve it? To the religious mind, of course he can. He's God. He can do anything.

Actually, he doesn't even need to be all-powerful, because if he isn't, the human mind will lend him a hand by anyway convincing itself that he is—which shows that the mind, too, can display some pretty impressive powers.

Demonstrations of irrationality in religion ordinarily don't much trouble the religious, yet they often enjoy riposting that the prime example of supposed rationality—science—is also pretty irrational at times.

They may mention, for example, *i*, the imaginary square root of minus one, which is as hard to form a mental portrait of as many of the esoteric things religions can dish up. Or they may say that in quantum physics a particle is simultaneously a wave, and vice versa. So, they may charge that the unity of wave and particle is just as mystical as that of Father, Son and Holy Ghost, and ask what's the difference between believing in one and believing in the other.

However, there are at least two problems with these accusations they may level against supposedly rational science.

The first is that (perhaps because they are frequently based on popularizations of science rather than on the hard science itself) they misunderstand what science actually *says* in each of the instances. For example, physics doesn't really say that a particle is simultaneously a wave. That's just a facile approximation. It's closer to the truth to say that there is something there—a quantum entity—which, depending on what tests it's put to, behaves either like a particle or like a wave. As for the square root of minus one, mathematical science uses it because it's a highly useful tool, not because scientists believe that imaginary numbers are at the same time—mystically—also real.

The second problem with the accusations is that they misunderstand what science really *does*. If this is cleared up, it isn't even really necessary to explain each individual misunderstanding, as with the particle/wave duality, in order to rebut the accusations.

Science does not believe in *anything* in the sense of "believing" that religion uses. In fact, nothing is scientific at all unless it is open, at least in principle, to being refuted.

The merest wisp of a tenet in a religious creed is stronger than the mightiest of scientific laws, because it's not to be questioned under any circumstances, even in principle (especially not in principle!)

Why do we feel the need for the psychological compensation that the gods provide for our own manifest weakness? Why don't we accept all our limitations as facts of life, and get on with it?

There is a simple answer, albeit the recognition may be hurtful: vanity.

Human vanity seems a veritable motherlode of motivations that lead to religious impulses. The Bible is wise—though quite beyond the way it intended—when it sees vanity everywhere…*vanitas vanitatum, et omnia vanitas.*

In a deeper sense, the concept of "vanity" doesn't really give final answers to the question of religiosity. One could ask, in turn, why humanity tends to have that trait. However, for present purposes it's valuable to bring it up simply as it manifests itself in practice. Another point: vanity has to be distinguished from a wish for self-improvement—which is laudable—although the two may mingle.

The word "vanity" may, unfortunately and unintentionally, sound insulting to those affected. They may not consider themselves in the least vain; in other areas of life they may indeed be devoid of any vanity. Yet they do consider it self-evident that—

for example—there *has* to be a destiny that makes it its business to oversee their life, or that makes sense of their existence, or gives it a purpose. (They need it; therefore, they think it *has* to be so.) And they quite fail to see this as an assumption that things are geared to them. That assumption is redolent of vanity.

One specific feature of much religious thinking (as always, in the broadest sense of "religious") is very clearly derived from vanity.

It is the disparagement, or downright rejection, of the element of chance in human affairs. The greater the importance that people, consciously or not, assume they have in the scheme of things, the less can they admit that there could be a lack of aim, of point, to anything that happens to them, or in fact to the world around them. If things happen "just because," it means we're contingent, not put here "for a purpose"—and that hurts.

On the other hand, if one has abandoned the idea that all events are governed by gods, all-seeing fates, or superstitions, chance must necessarily be seen to be not only logically possible, but factually everywhere. Yes, some things are governed by laws; the gravitational force isn't any chance figure, it's inversely proportional to the square of the distance. And yet, the law itself *could* have been "the *third* power of the distance" (or some other number); the consequences might have been dire, but it *could* have been so. At the ultimate root, everything is chance. We *could* still be amoebas; the falling cornice that killed So-and-So *could* have missed him by an inch. We can only be thankful that the former didn't happen and regret that the latter did.

That certainly doesn't mean that everything we can't find the reason for is the product of chance—which would be the opposite extreme. There may be some established natural chain of causes and results that we haven't discovered. Or an event that may strike us as pure happenstance could have been set up by some friend or enemy as a surprise, gag or covert attack. But after covering for all such cases, chance—pure luck, bad luck, or indifferent luck—remains.

"Nothing," said Leibnitz, advocating the opposite standpoint, "happens without a reason why it should be so, rather than otherwise." If what he meant is that no particle in the universe suddenly up and does something that violates the laws of nature, such as the latter happen to be, hardly anybody would dissent. But Leibnitz surely meant to make a much stronger statement than that. I can at this moment move my hand either to the left or to the right; neither action violates the laws of nature; not being a believer, I am not persuaded that when I do either, even this trivial choice is necessarily dictated by a reason (even one that remains unknown to me). Did Leibnitz mean to go so far? It would seem so.

One of the problems (and attractions) of philosophy is this; even with the apparently most clear-cut statements by philosophers, one has to ponder how literally they meant them. Not that establishing precisely what they meant implies that one then has to go by it. It's nice, and may be important, to know what Socrates said to Thrasymachus one fine morning, or what Adorno said to Horkheimer one blustery afternoon. But eventually, after incorporating as much of such knowledge as we want, each of us has to work out what *we* say on any issue that we care deeply about.

But don't take my word for that, either.

Having a sober, balanced assessment of our real worth and position is absolutely fundamental for broaching the Big Questions in life.

We do not matter cosmically; we do matter to ourselves and to our loved ones. We aren't godlike; neither are we an insignificant atom. Nor are we (at least in most cases!) despicable vermin only worthy of humiliating and punishing ourselves. We have to strike a balance—in this as in everything else in human affairs—and it helps if we don't delude ourselves about our standing.

So much about vanity, brought up as one reason for religiosity: religion assuages it. But of course religion does much more than that for believers. It provides superpowers and other goodies by proxy: our gods, at least, have what we cannot have ourselves. It may even provide some of the goodies directly to us, for example if, within the religion we believe in, immortality isn't only for the gods but for ourselves too in some way (like having a soul that lives on).

Here follows a list of some other things that religion does.

Religion provides what its believers hold to be answers and certainties.

It consoles in the face of personal loss, cosmic ignorance, etc.

It gives mystical delight.

It offers the gratification and/or relief that practitioners demonstrably derive from praying, from worshipping superior beings.

It provides ready-made rules of behavior; in that sense, it eliminates individual responsibility (which can be felt as a heavy burden) for one's positions on difficult issues, like abortion, etc.

It can deliver actual highs. This is why many religious people who are unable to work themselves up into one of these highs by the ordinary means of prayer, contemplation, etc., resort to physical means that can create the same result in the brain. These means may range from fasting, through self-torture of many kinds including strong whirling, to actual hallucinogenic drugs.

It offers a channel for self-loathing, self-abasement.

It offers a channel for those seeking to feel holy.

It offers a channel for those seeking to unburden or sublimate feelings ranging from guilt to power delusions.

It allows expression for a wish for martyrdom. Or for living as an anchorite. Or for achieving a feeling of community.

It supplies the ruling classes with a literally heaven-sent instrument of social control.

It gives clergies specific instruments for their own control over people, particularly in the case of religions that make it their business to dictate on people's sex lives.

It offers the tingle of delving into mysteries, of seeking (or even of achieving, as some practitioners will believe) some esoteric knowledge or power.

It offers participation in majestic ceremonials, simultaneously capable of making the self-important feel grand and the self-deprecating feel satisfyingly minuscule and awed.

It gives employment to vast numbers of people.

It offers hope in desperate circumstances.

It bestows a cloaking of good intentions on actions, like some military campaigns, that also have baser motives like seeking territorial gain or whatever.

It bestows a cloaking of otherworldly justification for the domination that some peoples exercise over others, particularly those they have defeated in war.

It bestows, at the moment of each religion's creation, a cloaking of otherworldliness to what may be, to a major degree, a political program of some type.

It gives diverse groups a feeling of being special as a people.

It provides help against enemies and other dangers, as when a tribesman wears an amulet, or a chaplain blesses an army before battle.

It provides a means for acting on a recalcitrant nature, as when people pray for rain. Or make sacrifices to the gods to seek protection for their herds. (With regard to this, it is, as many observers have noted, no wonder that a spread of agnostic worldviews in the West should have taken place as more people were more generations away from the herding of cattle and tilling of the soil. When technology allowed the world to be less rural, it made more bodies available for military campaigns; but it did more than that. It shook the pillars of the temple.)

The above list is impressive. No wonder religion has been so successful in finding and keeping believers.

CHAPTER 6
YES, BUT...

Here come the buts. Objection No. 1: religion is false.

The fact that religion offers all those benefits to its believers, that it satisfies all those yearnings, doesn't in itself make it true—just useful.

Religion does affirm its truth, of course, and with extreme vigor; but that truth, when pursued, boils down to the following dialogue:

"What I believe about my gods is true."

"How do you know it's true?"

"Because my gods told me so."

The same formula could be used for belief in absolutely anything. Remember my ytreqs? I'm convinced they exist, and account for my fate: an ytreq told me so himself! Religion is false because its "answers" to human concerns are either grounded, if one digs far enough, on circular, self-complacent reasoning, or its "proofs" could be used to demonstrate things it doesn't want to, too, which renders the reasoning useless.

The latter failing even applies to reasonings far more artful than the above "my gods themselves told me so." One of the most ingenious cogitations in religion is the so-called ontological argument of the existence of God, thought up by Anselm of Canterbury. God necessarily exists, he stated, because by definition he must have all the good attributes it's possible to have, and "existing" is one of the best possible attributes, so he has it. In fact existence is an attribute which God, in order to *be* God, can't be without.

This seems not only clever but unassailable, although by the time of Hume there already were many people busying themselves with trying to find some flaw in Anselm's reasoning. Nevertheless, it isn't really necessary to refute it "from within," i.e. by analyzing what it says. It can be fatally subverted "from outside," without any reference to its inner workings. All that's needed is to show that anyone can apply that same reasoning to demonstrate the existence of other, different beings that contain or even parody the idea of God. I'll do it right here: I conceive my ytreqs as the most wonderful thing possible, and existence is one of the most wonderful qualities there are, so they couldn't very well lack it, could they? Ergo, they exist.

With this, Anselm's effort to prove the existence of God stops making sense: it allows even ytreqs to make the grade.

Nor could a supporter of the ontological argument wriggle out of this *reductio ad absurdum* by saying that ytreqs are really God under another name, a different expression of the same absolute underlying truth, or some such formula. Ytreqs, as you may remember (or very likely don't), have essential differences, especially the fact that they're not creators.

Anselm's isn't the only apparently unassailable argument that religion holds in its quiver. Here is one from Krishna: "I never manifest [myself] to the foolish or unintelligent." Ignore the insult; let just the circularity remain. "If you don't believe in me, then, even supposing you have doctorates from Oxford, the Sorbonne and M.I.T., you are a fool and lacking in intelligence—and the proof of that is that you don't believe in me." Here again, even if you can't defeat the argument, you can outflank it, just by noting that ytreqs, also, don't manifest themselves to fools and the unintelligent.

Someone might yet object, "Krishna may well exist even if his argument is circular." Yes, and that could be extended: everything that religion affirms might be true even if ultimately resting on circular argumentation. From an agnostic standpoint, however, circularity, like inner contradiction, renders an argument pointless and false. And as always, if people anyway want to believe in it or the consequences derived from it, it's because of just that—

they want to. We atheists realize that wanting to believe something does not make it true.

End of story as regards falsity.

Falsity is a decisive point if there ever was one. But there's more. Objection No. 2: religion is, also, dangerous.

In fact religion presents at least three different perils.

(a) It has proven, over and over again, that it regularly drives people to horrible wars, persecutions and atrocities. People certainly start wars and commit atrocities for other reasons too, but that's no justification. Besides, it has an evident capacity to make people not just angry but wildly so (even pointing out to some religious people that religion can make people wildly angry wildly angers them); its wars and atrocities are among the most bloodthirsty of all.

I do recognize, of course, that some religions have a more bloodthirsty history than others. Still, it may be noted that even Zen Buddhism, which normally enjoys a wholesome image as the realm of contemplative monks and mountain sages with merry eyes, actually was an active supporter of the horrifyingly cruel Japanese militarism. A leading Japanese Zen sect in Japan admitted this and made a public apology. (More than half a century later, yes, but let's admit that this is far faster than what it generally takes the Roman Catholic Church to admit its own mistakes that have led to suffering and deaths, and there are other religions that never apologize at all.)

(b) Religion is also dangerous intellectually, because, by offering readymade but spurious "answers" to legitimate questions about the world and its workings, it hinders the search for better answers, i.e. real ones.

The hindering can take two forms. One is quenching legitimate curiosity. But in addition, if someone's curiosity persists anyhow, religion is quick to recognize a search for other answers as a huge threat, and tends to actively combat it, not hesitating to use the most violent, brutal means, such as burning people alive, or stoning them for heresy.

(c) And in the third place religion is dangerous because, whatever its original intentions—even if a particular creed was born revolutionary—it tends to turn, as alluded to earlier, into a tool of social control and domination.

In fact, with the second and third reasons acting together, historically religions have been, once established, overwhelmingly a reactionary force, generally opposed to change—any kind of change, not only in beliefs but in society, in the arts, in medicine, in any sphere of human life—out of principle. They may accept the changes in the long run, but kicking and screaming, and always too late.

Defenders of religion often counter such charges with the argument that one should not confuse religion with the actions of its fallible human practitioners.

There is no reason to fall for this argument. It is tempting to quote religion back at them: a tree, it says in the Bible, is known by its fruit (the exact quote is "wherefore by their fruits ye shall know them.") You can also make this point using words from secular usage—if it moves like a duck, if it quacks like a duck...

Of course, we know that appearances can be deceptive, and the line about the duck is a popular saying, not a proof. The real proof that believers are mistaken, if they claim one can separate religion from the behavior of the persecutory, intolerant and reactionary religious people found throughout its history, comes from the sadly overwhelming size of the accumulation of indications to the contrary.

If being dangerous is what religion again, again and again does—and we have thousands of years of experience to go by—then, I'm afraid, this is what religion *is*, whatever it proclaims on paper.

Believers may imagine a pure religion in the sense of an abstract entity separate from the people who practice it. Imagining, and giving credence to, ideal things of this type is, after all, what they do, as believers. Those of us who are outside their system of belief recognize that such an abstraction, the separation of religion from the religious, is nothing but a delusion, a chimera.

Of course religion can also be a force for good; it has led many people into noble, altruistic acts. But the cost of that, in terms of the bloodthirstiness it has historically unleashed in so many others, is too high. Just *one* person tied to a post and burned alive for religious reasons would have made the cost too high, because there is no reason to assume one can only have the good things if the bad ones are also accepted. The altruistic human traits that cause religion, in some cases, to be a force for good, can also be channeled in secular ways; more on that later.

Not opposing religion "because people also kill for other reasons" would be a bit like not opposing murder and terrorism because many people also die in car crashes.

Religion is one channel for many people's aggressive or socially censorious nature. There are others, like greed, racism and power mania. What helps is to try to block such channels when it's possible to do so. One propitious place to work on is religion, for being so often a channel for a murderous fervor that in addition is false, only offering transparently ad hoc and spurious answers to the issues it considers settled. Blocking those dangerous channels can be done, as is proven by the relative progress, through legislation and education, that some societies—those that are interested in doing so—have achieved against the racism that also seems innate and endemic in human nature.

Please note that none of the above charges against religion are against its occasional *corrupt* versions. They're not about fat-cat prelates or simony or negligently allowing the tribe's sacred fire to go out. They are about *inherent* falseness and dangerousness.

These two latter objections are so overwhelming that nothing else can really be necessary, and it seems almost like frivolity to additionally mention an objection that is, in effect, about esthetics. It's like saying, after arguing that a venerable but no longer salvageable building had better be torn down because it doesn't really offer the protection the people inside it believe it does—and is downright dangerous because jagged edges and falling pieces frequently injure and kill its inhabitants—that it's also painted in questionable taste.

Still, to make the record complete, here is the additional objection.

All religions arose, or at least have their original roots, in long-ago periods, when the majority if not all of their followers were at an early, low stage of sophistication. Therefore they quite naturally tended to go heavy on ceremonies, rituals and costumes with ornate visual and other effects intended to impress and awe people at that stage of development. Now they're still encrusted with bombast and gaudiness. These still clearly meet a need for many followers, but many others would recoil from them as embarrassing hocus-pocus, as well as sheer kitsch in visual terms, if they came across them in any other context of their lives.

There is an argument that the smoke and paraphernalia, the strange hats and clothing, the ponderous tones of voice that are employed, are *not* intended to awe the simple-minded, but to act as an aid in reaching a transcendental state of mind. However, that isn't much different: if external stimuli are needed it's just as bad as having a need for awe—a true inner conviction should be enough. And furthermore, skeptics may suspect that "a transcendental state of mind" essentially means a state of higher receptivity to flim-flam and snake oil—not, again, receptivity to inner conviction.

In my personal experience—which includes debates with everybody from a Mormon Temple Square guide in Salt Lake City, Utah, to a Brahmin in the holy city of Varanasi (old Benares) along the Ganges, in India, and an Islamic mullah in the equally-but-differently holy city of Bukhara, in Uzbekistan—when believers are confronted with the above arguments over falsity and over dangerousness, around here the conversation reaches the point where, at best, they may shake their heads and say:

"Well, whatever—but even *if* there's something in what you claim, which I'm not saying I admit, I anyway *want* to continue believing, *want* to continue practicing my religion."

To which the answer is: "Of course, by all means, go ahead! Believe and venerate anything you want, wear any costumes you deem appropriate, rattle whatever objects you hold sacred. (Just don't impose it on others. Please!)"

There is an interesting secondary matter that might as well be fitted in here. It concerns the phenomenon of people who, facing the world's beauty and complexity, are overcome by an experience that they describe as religious, although it doesn't feature any supernatural beings in it.

A few things may be pointed out concerning this. The first is semantic, regarding the use of the word "religious." For some people it may indeed be religious, but for others, if they weren't believers to begin with, when this feeling of intense awe washes over them they may only be using that word for lack of another, better one that describes it without the usual connotations that religiosity has. They might, for instance, experience enormous wonderment at the world without any accompanying reverential feelings. If they then say "religious" they may be stretching the meaning of the word a bit too much.

A second point to note is that while some people find the complexity, in particular, of the world to be a source of marvel, it can equally well strike others as absurd. Any engineer who designed anything with such layers upon layers, and then further layers and layers, of complexity as the anatomy and especially the physiology of, say, a mouse, would be locked up and kept away from sharp objects.

A third—the most important point—is that people's wonderment at the beauty of nature is usually selective, and that this affects the entire question. The Grand Canyon is normally seen as beautiful; a bog with rotting vegetation, which is equally natural, is "ugly." A kitten, oooh! One of those wiggly hairless creatures known as naked mole-rats, yuck!! The question arises, why doesn't this turn the religious urge on and off?

One final issue for this chapter. I certainly wouldn't want to find myself accused of avoiding it. It's the charge that atheism, too, has a history of violence. Two distinctions, and then I promise to deal with this matter head-on.

In general the book uses the words "atheism" and "agnosticism" interchangeably because it refers to both phenomena alike, but in this instance the difference between them, which is immaterial for other matters, is significant. In broad terms, atheism means not believing in a god or gods, and agnosticism means *acting* as if gods don't exist, whether they do or don't. With this in mind, atheism *may* or may not work people up into violence the same way that religion does; whether it does or not is a factual matter. Agnosticism, on the other hand, cannot, by definition.

Far am I from saying, of course, that agnostics are "better people" than atheists, or any such nonsense. For that matter, it should be clear that I have never said that nonbelievers, of whatever kind, are "better people" than believers, except if they are more tolerant. My position is that *all people* have some potential for violence inside them. And that some things (like, say, the protection of one's children) are more strongly conducive than others to making people violent. And, finally, that religious belief is among the worst in that regard.

The second distinction is between being anti-religious and being anti-clerical. Some of the most notorious cases of violence against religious people and buildings, notably in the French and Mexican Revolutions, have had anti-clericalism as a principal ingredient. (This was because the clergy had in both cases been a strong pillar of the repressive political regimes that the revolutionaries were attacking). One can be a *believer* and be anti-clerical. Thus, it's unfair to assign the blame for some incidents of violence against religious people and facilities to atheists if they were perpetrated for mainly anti-clerical reasons.

Of course, the overwhelming majority of murders of prelates and cases of destruction of temples, throughout history, were perpetrated by none of the above—neither by atheists nor by anti-clerical believers—but by fanatical followers of *other* prelates.

There remain the violent incidents that were indeed perpetrated by authentic atheists, which are the incidents that I promised to deal with head-on.

My first consideration is that any such cases must be categorically condemned, no ifs or buts. My personal position is that religious people must be allowed the freedom to believe and even to proselytize their belief. And that non-believers must, by the same token, be allowed the freedom not to believe and even to proselytize non-belief, just as energetically if they want to. But neither side has the right to employ coercion or violence. If, for example, one side considers that the other is engaging in dubious practices that amount to buying allegiance, for instance with free social services for the needy and free meals for those who attend their meetings, the proper way to counter this is by offering better inducements through their own institutions, not by resorting to coercion or violence.

The second consideration is that no acts of violence by one side are justified by the fact that the other side may engage in violence too. It's no excuse for the violence inherent in religion if atheists are or can be violent too.

The third consideration is that we actually have relatively few data to work on when sitting down to consider the phenomenon of atheist violence. Most of humanity has been religious in one way or another throughout history, so actions by atheists—actions of any type, including both pacific and violent ones—have necessarily been far less numerous than those involving religious people.

The fourth consideration is that, even among those examples of proven atheist violence, there have been no major ones in which atheism acted separately from other drives. In the most notable occurrence of all, namely the murderous Soviet anti-religious drives under Stalin, religion and the clergy were certainly persecuted on ideological grounds, being seen as purveyors of obscurantism, but simultaneously also as a political danger to the system. None of this is any justification for even a single assassination or persecution committed on atheism's behalf. But to do what we were trying to do—compare religion and atheism as triggers for violence—it would be most meaningful to compare episodes having them as sole motive. Religious mayhem, too, is often mixed with political or other drives. Yet we can also find countless occurrences in which religion, *as a sole drive*, has turned people violent, against other believers or against non-believers. Not so with non-belief.

The fifth and last consideration is that, since this involves an attempt to compare numbers, if a day comes in which, through new events, enough data have accumulated for the comparison to be statistically significant (and let's hope such a day never dawns), it will be necessary to compensate the figures mathematically to take into account the size of the involved populations. It makes no sense to consider two events, in each of which two hundred people were killed, as totally equivalent, if in one case two hundred were almost the entire population of a group and in the other the group was thousands or millions strong.

There simply isn't enough statistical evidence to make a true call. But since the issue is not to be ducked anyway, I'll make a call based at least on an impression. It's that, in view of the gigantic spasm of Hindu-versus-Muslim violence that accompanied the partition of India and Pakistan in 1947, religious violence far outdistances atheist violence in both relative and absolute terms. At the very least, the 1947 horror should by rights cause believers to pause before facilely equating the two kinds of violence. It would seem that the only sense in which they are equal is that they are equally to be condemned.

CHAPTER 7
DO THE BIG QUESTIONS IN LIFE REQUIRE RELIGION?

Maybe it didn't need to happen the way it did. Maybe when people first evolved the capacity to ask themselves major questions about the meaning, origin and destiny of the universe, about the foundation for ethics, etc., they might have gone straight to seeking secular, rational approaches to them, without turning to magic, religion and so on.

Still, it's doubtful that they could have done so at that point in history, and anyway it didn't happen. For that reason, when this book held that one of the springboards for belief was the need for answers to the Big Questions, it did so because this is what actually happened in mankind's history. A lay approach was possible in theory, but not *historically* possible, or at least likely.

However, now is the time to point out that there is nothing inherently religious about the questions. In fact, because they are reasonable questions (even if some of them turn out, upon examination, to be posed in unreasonable ways), in principle one might think they are better suited to answers derived from reason than from revelation. This is why they can be dealt with in entirely agnostic terms.

Why the questions did, in actual practice, receive a religious treatment first is quite clear. At the prehistoric stage of human history in which the Big Questions arose, people still hadn't developed the mental software to deal with them in other ways. Otherworldly answers are easier and virtually immediate. I can develop a whole system of answers involving my ytreqs in an afternoon, even if it may take some more time to establish the ytreqs' precise genealogies, the exact rites that need to be performed to venerate them, and the sacrifices that will help to mitigate their dangerous mood swings. Cavemen probably took longer to do the equivalent thinking ("there is a spirit in my axe, and it's stronger than the spirit in the mastodon, but still, better propitiate the spirit of the mastodon too"). Yet even so, it was much faster and mentally less taxing than trying to develop exclusively rational approaches. By the time the Greeks did hone the necessary mental processes (well, *some* Greeks did, whom the others preferred to force to drink hemlock, or to banish), otherworldly systems were firmly established—and with them the habit itself of turning to the supernatural when in search for answers. And these habits are so tough to be weaned from. A full 2,500 years later, most of mankind still hasn't done it.

Besides, there were the other drives, listed in chapter 6, that helped lead to the establishment of systems of belief—notably the drive to worship—and they reinforced one another.

CHAPTER 8
LAY OR ATHEIST?

As briefly intimated earlier, there is a distinction between a lay approach to issues, and an atheist approach to them, and this distinction between "lay" and "atheist" is—sometimes—important.

In an atheist approach, the supernatural is denied, rejected. Period.

Then there is the approach that can be called lay, or also secular, or agnostic. Nuances may be also distinguished between these latter three words, but for the purposes of this book's discussion they need not be gone into, because they make no difference to what is being driven at. In this specific regard they're like the distinctions between "supernatural" and "otherworldly," for example. They are here used interchangeably, just for variation.

The lay/secular/agnostic approach doesn't say the supernatural exists and it doesn't say it doesn't. It excludes it; it *acts as if* it didn't exist.

Modern human societies, for example, are secular (or they aren't modern) but they are certainly not atheist. This is one example of a place where the distinction between agnostic and atheist is important. Many or most people in these societies are privately religious to some degree, which is why these societies are not atheist. But they are secular because religion is not allowed to be brought (too much, and at least so far) into public life.

Now, for the particular needs of most of the arguments in this book, the distinction between secular and atheist is *not* important. That is why in such cases it uses these words interchangeably, again simply for purposes of variation.

Note anyway that, when the distinction matters, being atheist necessarily includes being agnostic, but being agnostic doesn't necessarily imply being atheist.

One word distinction that does remain crucial is between different senses of the word "lay" itself. "Lay Jews" are Jews who don't believe in God, but maintain that if they keep up their cultural and ethical heritage they're "just as good Jews" as those who are strictly orthodox in religious terms. (In fact, I personally would add—under the terms of that very heritage—that if they're more tolerant they're even *better* Jews). This is open to much debate—it refers, after all, to religion—but the fact is that this is how lay Jews use the word. "Lay Christians" means exactly the opposite; it means people who believe, and strongly—so strongly that they work to assist the clergy, without being clergy themselves.

Lastly, notice also that there is one sense of the word "agnostic" that this book prefers *not* to employ, that of simply "skeptical" or "doubting." The book's agnostics have already decided to ignore the supernatural or rule it out.

These considerations end the "whereas" part of the book. Now we turn, one by one, to life's Big Questions, and to related smaller questions.

PART II: HOW?

CHAPTER 9
THE MEANING OF LIFE

What is the meaning of life?

A heavyweight question. And it can be answered. However, first it's necessary—and easy—to clear away a built-in assumption hidden within the question. The next step is to dispose of some meanings of the word "meaning" that can also cloud the issue, if one isn't alert. Do that, and the path to grappling with it in a thoroughly agnostic manner is almost automatically visible.

(One more thing: it should be noticed that talk about the meaning of life usually refers to a meaning that "comes" with life, that's built into it, not a meaning that *we* endow our life with—for instance when we dedicate our life to a cause).

The straightforward, customary phrasing of the question—"what is the meaning of life?"—contains an unspoken prior assumption. Stated brutally: it takes it for granted that life *has* a meaning. That assumption could be right; it could be wrong—but either way, it cannot be left unexamined. So, we first have to broach the more basic question, "does life necessarily have a meaning?"

If you are a nonbeliever, in the religious sense, by definition you have no expectation that a superior being of some sort created you, created life, or created the universe itself. Somehow, those things happened (see the chapter on "the origin of everything," below)—but the main thing is that they didn't happen in a supernatural way.

And that being the case, the agnostic answer clearly is that no, there is no reason to assume or expect that life has a meaning—*except that the phrase "life has no meaning" itself has several meanings, and one of them is that "life is not worth living," and that is patently not the case.* Read on.

Thus, when life appeared, it didn't *necessarily* come with an attached meaning. It could, of course, have one anyway, because many things that aren't necessary nevertheless patently exist; just watch what's on TV.

And so, back to the initial question: *does* life have a meaning anyway, even if having one wasn't a necessity? Again, for a nonbelieving mind the answer springs easily. "No; as with God himself, we're not in the business of positing the existence of things—in this case, a meaning for life—on no more real basis than that it might be soothing to have them exist."

(In yet another turn, it could still be objected that such things might yet exist unknowably even if *we* find no reason to believe that they actually do. Haven't we been here before? The answer is: yes, of course they might—but so might fairies, or ytreqs.)

In sum, here's an atheist's answer to the first Big Question. It's straightforward. Hurtful, undoubtedly, to some; simply accurate and realistic, to others. Life doesn't *have* a meaning, *in the religious sense* of "meaning." However—and it's a big however—the word "meaning" has other senses too, so in important other senses you can find a meaning if you want to. That's what we look at next.

The last thing this book wants to do is engage in unnecessary semantics and hair-splitting. In this case, however, it really helps if we distinguish among some different "meanings of meaning." In the very phrase "the meaning of meaning," the word is already being used in two different senses, though that's pretty evident. In other cases, such clarity isn't necessarily the case. The question of the meaning of "meaning" threatens such circularity that it's like Bill Clinton's "what 'is' is" all over again. However, that doesn't imply that it's unsolvable for practical purposes.

"Meaning" can variously mean "definition of," "signification," "significance," "sense," "purpose," "gist," "value," "point." Some of the senses are closely related, others more distantly so, others not at all. That's why some people, when asking about the meaning of life, are really asking, "*why* do we live?" And some are asking, "is there a point to living?" And some, "is life worth living?" The questions may sound similar, particularly the last two, but aren't really the same. There may be a point to living, but who says we have to like that point? Or, we may decide that it certainly *is* worth living, the hell with its point or lack of it. (The latter happens to be my personal view, for what it's worth).

The conclusion that life doesn't have a meaning refers to its not having an inbuilt purpose or point—the teleological senses of "meaning." And if people have achieved a fairly sober estimation of their real importance in the overall scheme of things, in the universe (you may recall what was said about this in an earlier chapter), they have no reason to feel hurt or diminished by that conclusion. It does leave open our lives' meaning in the other senses: those of our value, of having a reason to live or not.

Our value is not conferred by others, much less by a superbeing—who can't do so because he, she or it doesn't exist—but by ourselves. There's nobody here but us to do it.

Life is just something that (thankfully) happens to be there, but it *is* there; so even in tough circumstances, make the most of it while you can.

In fact: if you've truly grasped that there was no reason for life to *have* a meaning in the first place, why should you miss this something that never had a reason to exist? But if you positively demand that life at least have a non-religious meaning, you can see life's meaning in the very fact that we can live it—a privilege that neither the inanimate nor the dead enjoy.

To some, like for instance me, to use the word "meaning" even as defined in these restricted terms already smacks of otherworldly strivings. But that's likely to be no more than a question of taste.

One can feel that the satisfactions of life itself—anything from one or two quiet moments alongside a loved person, pet or thing, on up—are great, even among its woes. Even if one doesn't, this recognition of the true situation has twin advantages that will emerge as central to this book. They are the advantage of knowing that one is not giving life a phony added significance based on otherworldly make-believe; and thus, secondly, the satisfaction of standing on one's own two feet. (That's a metaphorical phrase, and obviously not a put-down of the physically disabled; it simply means self-reliance.)

The above is, then, a totally agnostic attitude to the question of the meaning of life.

CHAPTER 10
HOW CAN YOU *LIVE* WITHOUT BELIEVING IN ANYTHING?

This is, as already mentioned in the first chapter, a question often asked of atheists, in some phrasing or another.

This question, too, is one of those that make a not-very-hidden prior assumption. Namely, in this case, that "people *need* to believe in something." The question isn't a straightforward request for information, like "how can I remove this stain from my shirt?" Much less is it a minor expression of envy or admiration, like "how can you park your car in so small a spot?" At heart the questioners are including their own answer, namely that it can't be done. Which is to say that rather than being a question, although it's shaped like one, it's a statement, viz. that if you say you can live without "believing in anything," you're wrong or deluded (maybe even worse, that you're morally challenged).

Happily, none of this means that the question can't be answered.

When one has been asked this question, a possible answer is that one can live without believing in anything (in the senses that the person who asked the question uses the words) by deriving satisfaction from the very fact of not requiring the support of illusory, ad-hoc beliefs in order to get through life, or, on a more positive note, in order to even enjoy life.

But even that sounds a bit too dependent. Not being mistaken is a negative accomplishment (even if it certainly *is* an accomplishment, considering how overwhelmingly widespread it has always been to make the mistake of believing illusory things).

On a more positive note, then, here is an answer. One can live without believing in anything because one realizes (a) that the satisfactions of the world itself (including those of the mind, of course, and other equally intangible *but not otherworldly* satisfactions) are enough to sustain one through life, and (b) that the woes of the world can be borne by one's own inner resources too.

At this point, the questioner may try to complain that this isn't a real answer but a specious one, because, boiled down, it says that "one can live without beliefs because one can."

But it's a bit more subtle than that. The answer says that if one stops taking it for granted that outside beliefs are necessary to sustain one, and if one examines what actually happens when one gives them up, one makes the discovery, a factual one, that one's own inner resources are indeed sufficient for the task. (There may also be the help of other people, why not—help through something they say or do, or just from their being there—but getting help from other people, or giving it to them, was already part of what was meant by the above phrase "the satisfactions of the world itself.")

Which is what we were trying to get to, as far as nonbelievers are concerned.

Yet the questioner may doggedly insist that the second version still is nothing but a (now even better hidden) version of "it works because it works." There is also an answer for that: Precisely! That's what we were saying all the time—it works because it works, and we are the living proof of it. But in the phrase "it works because it works," the second "it works" isn't just a willful statement, it's the result of an empirical observation—we look around and verify that one can indeed find some people, like for example ourselves, who do manage to live perfectly well without "believing in anything." And this encompasses living perfectly well (okay, as well as one can in this complex, not to mention expensive, world of ours) not only in a material but also in the non-religiously spiritual sense of the appreciation of beauty, the satisfactions of goodness and so on.

Incidentally, why is this particular belief, the belief that nobody can live without belief, so prevalent? Why do so many believers insist on it? I'd guess it's mainly the unwarranted extrapolation to everybody else of their feeling that *they* cannot live without belief. Plus, they seem to derive some sort of psychological satisfaction from making the extrapolation. Again, they may be trying to extract a confession that their interlocutor secretly does, after all, have some residual religious belief. In any case, what they are really saying is, "I believe you do believe in something." And this belief of theirs can be as unshakeable as their other ones. It's equally pointless to try to shake it.

To change tack, the questioner may say: "You've said that one of the main springboards for human otherworldly beliefs was vanity.

But what about you? To hold that you can manage perfectly well in life without the beliefs that sustain most other people is pretty vain, isn't it?"

I actually call it justifiable pride in standing on my own two legs; I don't really think it's vanity at all. Still, if I call my learned opponent's position "vanity" and my own position "justifiable pride," I have to take it with good grace if he or she does it the other way around. Fair's fair.

Another reason I can take it with good grace is that, let's face it, nonbelievers have been called a lot of worse things than "vain."

CHAPTER 11
(NOT IN A BANKRUPTCY SENSE!)
THE ORIGIN OF EVERYTHING

A religious believer is on a vacation in India, say (a believer from somewhere else, of course), and tomorrow needs to take one of the trains from Agra to Jodhpur, but he doesn't know the departure times. (Let's suppose the believer is a he, for the sake of simplicity.) He has tried every available avenue to knowledge—the railroad's own information services, the concierge at his hotel, the Internet, other travelers, etc.—but they all either don't know or give him such conflicting data that he ends up just as unenlightened as before. He still doesn't know at what times the trains leave, and in fact is beginning to entertain the dangerous doubt if a train from Agra to Jodhpur exists at all.

In such circumstances, does he conclude that, since he is unable, at least for now, to find out the departure times—and may indeed, for all he knows, *never* be able to do so—the right thing to do is fill the void with an ad-hoc answer that satisfies his need to have some degree of certainty before he sets off for the railroad station? On the basis that *any* answer is better than *no* answer, does he search his soul, and for good measure mortify his body, until a certitude emerges from within him, and he looks up and exclaims, "Trains leave at 8 A.M., 1 P.M., and 7:15 P.M.!"

No? Then why would he adopt such a procedure for an immeasurably more important issue than a railroad timetable, like the origin of the universe, and base himself on an inner feeling of conviction to proclaim, "There are undetectable beings called gods, and they created it!"?

The above example may be criticized as too loaded. In reality, it's only a *reductio ad absurdum* of the procedure by which hard-to-answer or unanswerable questions about the universe have traditionally been "answered." And in actual fact, it's the traditional religious answers that are loaded, given that their affirmations about God are unanswerable, hopelessly circular—but let that pass in this instance.

Historically, when there were gaps in the available information, mankind has posited gods to fill them. As the gaps were gradually filled in, the gods receded—rain was first caused by a god, then the cycle of water was understood, and that god lost that job. Finally many gods essentially became rather abstract principles. Gods kept all their other functions—comfort, social control, etc.—but as answers for recalcitrant scientific conundrums they were only there as a very last resort.

How far has this process reached now? Today, at least in modern societies, the boundary is the following: God has retreated to just on the other side of the Big Bang.

Most people would be ashamed to catch themselves thinking that what caused the observable universe *to expand* was an act of

59

the will on the part of some deity. However, when they take their questioning just one step further, to what put the expanding universe there, they unblushingly maintain it definitely *was* such an action by a deity. In fact, in this, their gut feeling may be so vehement as to make them regard anybody who doesn't believe likewise as a bad person. Unworthy, for example, of holding high public office. (More on this in another chapter).

So, to this day, the gods remain in use for the Big Questions. And the procedure by which they got there is just as unwarranted as the insight that led to the powerful conviction, "8 A.M., 1 P.M., and 7:15 P.M.!"

Mankind's traditional procedure for answering the Big Questions also reminds me of the way that Sally Brown and Peppermint Patty, in the *Peanuts* comic strip, answer their multiple-choice quizzes at school (every book on philosophy must quote from the *Alice* books, Woody Allen, or *Peanuts*, and if possible from more than one of these three sources). Sally and Peppermint Patty never know the answers, but neither do they leave the quiz boxes unmarked. Rather, with a mixture of bravado and desperation, and of course cluelessness, they slash boldly, blindly ahead with their pencils, shouting, "X! 22! The Magna Carta!"

The agnostic way to approach the question where the world came from, or any other that's found to be unanswerable (whether we consider the unanswerability to be apparent or essential), is to *leave* it unanswered. We don't have an answer; but we do have an approach—namely that having no answer (either for the time being, or even forever) is better than having an unwarranted one.

We put the question on hold, however irksome that may be, because it's the only thing we can really do. Most people are satisfied by giving themselves the answer that the universe was the work of a supernatural being. We agnostics prize honest ignorance above spurious answer.

We may also ask whether "who created the universe?" is an honest question in itself, because it already loads the issue in terms of assuming that *someone* created it, and in fact it also assumes that it *was* created. Realizing this doesn't necessarily bring us a whit closer to an answer—except insofar as asking better questions is always an improvement.

Questions like those of origins are scientifically very difficult ones. Even if we assume that humanity will one day find the answers to them, it isn't reasonable to think that it should already have done so: scientific research has only been put on authentic foundations in very recent centuries. Non-believers are just as ignorant as everybody else on such unresolved matters. They simply value the fact of knowing they're more honest about it.

Related to the question of the origin of everything is the question of the ultimate reason there *is* anything. Why is there something when there could be nothing—no universe? The agnostic approach to this is the same. We just don't know; and we prefer this admitted ignorance to ad-hoc answers of the type, "God willed it so," or "an ytreq decided so."

Further, we think that the very phrasing "there could be nothing" subliminally prejudges the case.

CHAPTER 12
HOW ABOUT BELIEVING IN SOME ABSTRACT PRIME MOVER?

In debates with our theistic friends and acquaintances, we nonbe-lievers may have found from experience that the point is reached where they say something along the following lines.

"All right," they'll tell us, "suppose that you reject the entire concept of a personal god or gods who keep an eye on human destinies. For you, no pantheon, no angels, no archangels; for you, even if there are people who behave in a saintly way, there are no saints with supernatural powers. And, for you, no clerics, no revealed texts, no prayers to otherworldly powers; no gongs, bells, horns, or conches; no sacred trees, rocks, images, or beads. Still…"—and here comes the crunch—"do you agree at least that if there's a world, then something created it? Even if we don't agree on who or what it really was; even if we never get to know it; and even if we don't prejudge whether he, she, or it, was of a natural or supernatural character—even so, do you agree that surely *something* must have created what exists?"

"Well," we demur, "I'd start by not even agreeing with that way of phrasing the issue, since maybe it wasn't a creation at all, at least in the way we are able to conceive the term."

"Maybe—but we've got you anyway! You said 'the issue.' You admit there's an issue."

"Of course—I just don't want to prejudge it, I don't even want to get tied into any way of *talking* about it that may prejudge it."

"Okay, okay," they cut in. "Here's our point: if there's an issue, why not call the answer to the issue 'God'? It's just a name, a word!"

This is the question this chapter deals with.

"Just giving something a name" isn't always an innocent action. A name, any name, may turn out to be much more than an innocuous label for whatever it is we are talking about. Labeling can be powerful medicine; it conditions the way we think about the thing labeled.

And if a name *must* be given, "God" would be the very last one we'd be well advised to adopt.

"God" comes with built-in connotations of something or someone to venerate, obey, appeal to, appease, etc. Above all, we are ripely familiar with God as a supernatural, not a natural entity, so that any acceptance of that name would *presuppose* a supernatural answer. This is so obvious that if we didn't know our friends better, we might even suspect that our intelligence is being insulted when they make an attempt to pass "God" off as "just a name, a word."

So, thanks, but no thanks.

But then comes a follow-up. "All right," they'll say to us nonbelievers, "let's not use the word 'God.' Let's use a completely neutral word or phrase. How about 'Ultimate Cause'? No—we can tell from your faces that you're going to object that even this is too strong." (It is—it makes the assumption that there *were* causes afoot, and not, maybe, just a happenstance without causes, and furthermore, that among the causes there was one that was the ultimate one).

"All right," they pursue, "why not just call it 'the answer'? Or even 'the something'? Or let's not use words at all! Why not give it an entirely abstract name like 'R9,' for example?"

The wisest answer is, "No, we're not falling for that trap either." Even something as vague as "the something" or "R9" cannot help but lead back to the same situation. We cannot avoid knowing that "R9"—whatever it is—is what we owe our existence to. And sooner or later—probably rather quickly—we'll be right back where we were, with thankfulness, then veneration, fear, appeasement, the lot.

Some people may bring up here that they think that venerating something, etc., is good or even necessary for people. That's dealt with in another chapter.

So, nice try, but again no, thanks.

CHAPTER 13
IN THAT CASE, HOW ABOUT BELIEVING IN "THE FORCE"?

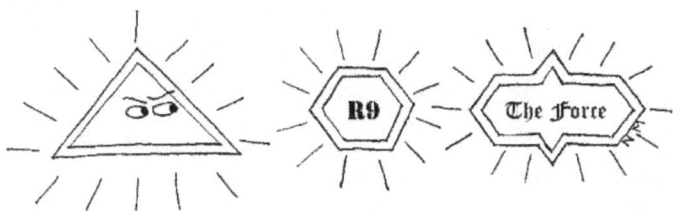

The next tack, after failing to convince us to accept some ineffable agency as Prime Mover, may be to try to get us to accept some equally ineffable energy or force as Current Operator of the universe.

"Forget the question of the creation," believers may argue. "Something must be running the universe *now*. And if you object to the term 'running,' it can be something more indefinite, perhaps a word like 'overseeing' or even just 'accompanying' or what you will. Exactly what it does doesn't matter, if it indeed it 'does' anything. But surely you feel that if there is no god, at least there's *something*—an energy, a force, a power—out there?"

Obviously they're not referring to something like the force of universal gravitation, or the anti-gravitational "dark energy" being investigated by astronomers, physicists and cosmologists. They mean a somehow metaphysical energy, not a grubbily physical one.

It's the idea used in George Lucas' *Star Wars* movies, with their woolly mysticism, albeit cinematographically a very effective one, revolving around what they called The Force. For a time, the movies' phrase, "May the Force be with you," enjoyed great popularity and dissemination.

To recap, the question was, "Surely you feel there is *something*—an energy, a force, a power—out there?" Here's an answer: if this is about what we *feel*, as the question puts it, then no, we feel no such thing. Nor do we see any rational grounds (the only grounds that interest us in these matters) for the existence of such a metaphysical energy, force or power.

What we *know* is that a lot of people do believe that kind of idea, though—that's an observable fact. And another is that "force" and "energy" and "power" are three terribly misunderstood, misused and abused concepts. Not that it makes any sense to demand that these words be used only in the strict senses they have in physics. But people do extrapolate so very wildly from those senses.

Sometimes this simply happens because they want to refer to something intangible for which they lack a better word, so they say "energy," "power" or "force" basically because these words are available. At other times they really seem to think they are making a valid extrapolation or analogy.

An example of wild extrapolations whose validity is still accepted by huge numbers of people: the moon demonstrably has the power to act on the water in the earth's seas, causing the tides (through gravitation); therefore, the moon has the power to affect our destiny (through who knows or cares what agency); therefore, further, *all* objects in the sky have the power to affect our destiny.

All manner of energies and forces are pressed into service for mental constructions built on factual quicksand. In the human body, electricity flows among cells, and human bodies have power, both muscular and intellectual. On the basis of this, the most carefree extrapolations are made about fields of force, powers and energies that envelop the bodies like an aura, or maybe, to the otherwise minded, are concentrated at special points. A *car* also has electricity flowing through it, and power, but no such extrapolations are made for it (except perhaps by feng shui enthusiasts. Things placed in one particular way may look better than in others, and this soothes the onlooker; charging ahead from this practical effect, feng shui practitioners become positively shamanistic in their belief in spiritual forces residing in objects.) But there is no valid reason to make any merrier extrapolations about humans, in this sense, than about cars.

It brings many people satisfaction to believe in mystical energies unknown to physics or physiology, or even to believe that they're real, physical ones. It's understandable, but it's arbitrary.

In view of the above considerations, sorry about the idea of getting us to accept an Energy hovering through the universe. No, thanks.

But we can anyway, as a nice gesture, tell our interlocutors, "May the Force be with you."

CHAPTER 14
THE SOUL

If "the soul" is understood in its developed religious senses, it's simply a non-issue for the truly non-believing.

If there's no religion, there's no soul. In point of fact (actually in point of logic), under that condition there *can* be no soul. End of story.

Things, of course, quickly get more complicated than that, because the term "soul" has been invested with such a wealth and jumble of meanings.

At the opposite extreme, "soul" is sometimes used just as an expression for what makes us *living* beings. Then we humans naturally do have souls, since we are alive. However, this meaning of the term, though we actually come across it sometimes, isn't really espoused even by those who employ it—as soon as they stop to think about it a bit. It gives a soul to every animal, to every last blade of grass, and they are seldom willing to go so far. Worse than that, it means we lose our soul the moment we die, a notion they tend to emphatically disapprove of.

Similarly with "soul" when it means something along the lines of "consciousness" or "self-awareness," which it sometimes does. Surely its proponents don't mean something that ceases to be when we are asleep, unconscious, drugged or in a coma, although this can be fixed by adding all the appropriate and necessary provisos to the definition.

If soul means simply "mind," of course we have a soul. This has the advantage that it doesn't get snuffed out when we go to sleep or are knocked out, but a soul that is merely the mind doesn't signify much from a religious standpoint, in part because then animals also get to have souls. Also, if having a soul just means having a conscience, then again: of course we have a soul.

The issue becomes progressively more vexed when all the other ideas subsumed under the word "soul" are brought into play or given free (even if unspoken) rein, which is normally the case. Namely, the soul as the alleged seat of spiritual and moral things, the soul as the essential part of something, including us (which, by the way, presupposes that such a thing as essentiality indeed exists, which can and has long been debated, but let's not go here into the question of essentialism), the soul as the seat of the emotions, and so on.

Do we have a life of the "spirit"? If that means whether human beings are moved by other interests than merely keeping fed, warm, and sexually satisfied at the simplest levels, then obviously everybody has a spirit (okay, almost everybody).

However, the proponents of the idea may mean something different. By "having a spiritual life" they usually also mean, or imply, that we have an ineffable substance-that-isn't-a-substance that—separate from the body but residing in it, at least until death—is the seat and the driving force of those spiritual pursuits.

In that case, they are just using "spiritual life" as tantamount to, or demanding, the usual, religious definition of soul. And in that case no, such things don't exist, say we non-believers. It's again a question of definition—if we thought we had one of those ineffable things, that would be precisely the kind of attitude that would define us as believers, not nonbelievers.

This can get very circular. But it's not *our* fault. The fault lies with positing, through faith, the existence of things whose consequences, once examined, turn out to be mutually, circularly interdependent as a way to keep the whole edifice of faith standing.

How did the idea of a soul arise? People noted a lot of complex phenomena—the fact of being alive, feelings of goodness, love for music and poetry, capacity for friendship, inchoate yearnings, self-awareness, emotions, etc.—with no obvious explanation or even a clear seat, the way a knee pain has its seat in the knee. There is an easy, time-tested way out: calling an answer into existence by giving the whole grab-bag a name. In this case, "soul."

Maybe the process wouldn't have been quite like this if it happened to unfold from scratch today, when we know a lot more about the brain and about psychology. Not that the brain is the answer to all the issues that the concept of soul addresses (and not that we fully understand the brain either); but the brain does offer another (and natural, not supernatural) interpretation of a number of the issues. In any event, that's not the way it happened, and the concept of the soul became firmly established.

About salvation: if there is no soul in the religious sense, there is no salvation issue. No soul is out there, or in there, requiring being saved. We have to live within the dictates (see the chapter on ethics) of the law and of our consciences—not a minor issue—and that's that.

CHAPTER 15
DEATH AND IMMORTALITY

Enjoying a thoroughly lay worldview—a worldview without any gods or other supernatural phenomena in it—can do several things for us, in terms of providing an approach to the issue of death. Here are four:

(1) It bases that approach on an unadorned understanding of our true biological position in the scheme of things. Knowing that this is so is a satisfaction in itself.

(2) Contrary to habitual expectations, lack of belief in God can actually make the fact of death easier to digest, rather than more difficult. It entirely frees us from the twisting and turning in the wind that believers endure when they seek to convince themselves there's some good reason why their basically beneficial God foisted death and other miseries on them.

(3) Thirdly, there is the satisfaction, a very basic and crucial one, of knowing that we are not facing our problems with spurious crutches, but standing up to them on our own two legs. And this even brings a bonus: the legitimate pride we may derive from such self-reliance is actually greater the greater the loss we are faced with.

(4) Having a lay worldview just dissolves all the fears and all the problems of the afterlife. But they are not dissolved like a puff of smoke in the wind, or like Count Dracula when the sunlight hits him, because the process is an even more powerful one: it's not a question of taking something that exists and making it vanish. What the lay worldview shows us is that there never was anything there in the first place.

In the face of death, we naturally experience grief. The above consolations may seem paltry by comparison, but they have a huge advantage over any apparently stronger ones that are based on an intervention of the supernatural: they are real. They may be small, but there is nothing phony about them.

Death can be inexpressibly sad. The death of loved ones, it goes without saying; and our own perhaps too. It's much more than merely having to leave so many dear people and things, and life itself, and unfinished projects. The dying replicant puts it beautifully in the movie *Blade Runner*: "I've seen things…you people wouldn't believe. Attack ships on fire off the shoulder of Orion…I watched C beams glitter in the dark near the Tannhäuser Gate…All those…moments…will be lost…in time…like…tears in the rain."

And these are just an android's feelings.

It should be evident, but it's worth stating explicitly, that a lay worldview cannot offer any ultimate consolation in the face of death. Death is indeed a terrible, devastating thing. (Save perhaps in the case of some abominable scoundrels whom we may suspect have it richly coming to them. As the Lord High Executioner sings in *The Mikado*, "They'd none of 'em be missed—they'd none of 'em be missed!")

But, on the other hand, the lay worldview does offer some considerations that can, to some extent, help us to bear death since bear it we must, anyway.

One absolutely fundamental element, which in fact lies at the heart not only of this section but of the entire book, is doing one's best to avoid vanity and thus to assess our real situation and importance soberly. If that's done—admittedly not an easy chore, by any means—one realizes that the warranted question is no longer "why do we have to die?" but "why shouldn't we have to?"

We may strongly rue the fact that we have chanced to appear in a chain of life that is organized on a basis of discardability of the individual. *But that's what happened*—that's where we appeared in the world's scheme of things.

Consider that it could be worse, because we could be like those other animals that lay thousands of eggs so that a just a few offspring may reach maturity. It could also, admittedly, be much better. Life could have been simpler, and far more secure.

But that's the way it is. Those are the facts; we must face the facts. Wittgenstein began his *Tractatus Logico-Philosophicus* with the statement, "The world is everything that is the case." He probably thought of this as crystal-clear, maybe in the sense of "There are no fairies—fairies aren't the case—so don't believe in them." In actual fact various things could be meant by the statement, which people still debate; some may even suspect that it hides a tautology. But one of the things Wittgenstein must definitely have meant is that we must not look in our world for things that are not the case; and in this, we can safely follow him.

This is our world, not a different one; and in it, the case is that everything that lives, dies. (All right, there are some arguable fringe cases. There is, for example, a plant by the name of *Welwitschia mirabilis* that lives solitarily and with shriveled tips in the Namib desert and seems to go on forever; there are some small organisms that reproduce by asexual cloning, or that periodically regress to a larval state and then regrow, about which it's still debated if they should be considered as having one life that's everlasting. But think about it. Who really wants to live forever half-shriveled in the Namib desert, or to be a tiny asexual creature or periodically be a larva?)

In this our world, some entities are endowed with life; and, at the end of life, comes death. It's that simple. Tough, too. But this is the case.

Now, beyond what was said in the previous paragraphs, the question, "Why do we have to die?" isn't even properly phrased. "Having" to do anything, in that sense, could be seen to imply the existence of some entity that does the commanding. Even seeing the question in terms of a "nature that has made things so" places the issue atop a slippery slope of anthropomorphic nature, teleology and, in the end, pantheism.

If we want to keep the gods out of things, there is a suitable way to handle questions of the type, "Why is this, or that, or the other, so in life?"

The procedure is to handle them the same way we handle questions like "Why does water flow down rather than up?" In other words, we seek to establish the natural causes, if we can, rather than chase metaphysical wherefores. This doesn't mean reducing everything to physics and chemistry, because things may also be due to complex psychological, sociological, economic or similar causes which are not reducible to physics and chemistry. But they're definitely not metaphysical.

Why *does* water flow down rather than up? Nobody, not even devout believers in God, nowadays answers that it does so because that was God's will (although some people still think that water can be controlled by supernatural agencies, given that they pray against floods or droughts). What we say instead is that water flows down because of gravity; and then either we can account for gravity in turn, or we can't. But, after great tribulations in the history of knowledge—and often against a bloody rearguard action by the established bodies of belief—we have realized that it's pointless to see that kind of question in terms tantamount to "*Who* arranged for water to flow down rather than up?" Much less does the question entail this other: "Did we do something bad that *caused* the choice to be down rather than up?" Let alone, "If we resolve to be good from now on, will water please, please flow up rather than down?"

Yet asking such questions is the otherworldly approach that most people don't see as at all laughable, when they apply it to other questions of the "why is this so in life?" type.

We may "feel" that the why of death is very different from the why of the direction of water flow. But in fact they both refer to facts of nature, and if there is a difference it's only that our own death, or that of a loved one, affects us more powerfully.

Psychologically, the approach outlined here will be of greater help to some people than to others. It cannot *wholly* comfort anyone, no matter what his or her psychology, in the face of his own death or that of a loved one. But it's all we have, if we have given up the gods as a perhaps handy but unwarranted support.

Believers include many gifted and subtle thinkers, and they've managed to come up with what to their eyes are answers that settle the question why a presumably beneficial deity created a system prominently featuring death, pain and loss. Those answers may be along the lines of the doctrine of original sin; or of the idea that pleasure cannot be conceived unless it's in opposition to pain; or that grim realities are included in God's deal just to keep us on our toes, or to make us tough. Or that cover-all standby— God's unfathomableness. Still, even if they won't admit it, the creators of such arguments are hard pressed when death comes to a clearly blameless infant. Unless they opt to believe (many do) that God is an incredibly rancorous entity still capable of punishing a baby for the sins of its forefathers, eons ago.

A non-believer doesn't need to enter any of this. Not believing in God, there is nothing that needs explaining about that kind of woe in the world. This world of ours happens to be the world that exists. Things are so. Yes, they could have been otherwise. But they weren't, so that's the way they are. It's a world in which many babies and many good young people die.

This most certainly doesn't mean we should accept everything dumbly and not try to improve things through medical, scientific and social discoveries and improvements that make our lives better. *Quite the contrary*—it is religion which has historically taught people to accept things as they are, has opposed changing things, and has tended to only accept scientific discoveries and medical improvements when forced to, grudgingly, with bad grace, and decades or centuries late.

One caveat: religion's difficulty in accounting for pain, for death, for evil, obviously only applies for a religious system with one god, who is additionally conceived as essentially good, even if stern. It won't work for religions with two or more gods, among whom there is at least one evil deity. Well, you can't win them all.

Religious systems, in the most general terms, are ad-hoc scaffoldings providing man with support and consolation in the face of his ignorance, fragility and mortality. Discarding these scaffoldings takes guts. But it needs to be done, just as a child needs to give up crawling on all fours, needs to abandon its walker, and get around on its own legs, even if there's a certainty of some hard knocks ahead. (For instance in thickets of metaphors such as this one).

But there's another way of looking at this process, too: it's not only necessary, it's utterly unavoidable if one has already seen through the hollow nature of the supports offered by supernatural beliefs. If we have, for whatever reason, stopped believing in the gods and in all the attendant fables, they obviously will no longer be able to generate the requisite feel-good factor.

So, in the face of bereavement, what can we do? We grieve. In the face of our own mortality, what can we do? We may rail, we may feel short-changed (we may know it for a fact, if we are relatively too young to die), we may go through the usual phases of denial et al. But, ultimately, we face it.

The awareness that we are coming to grips with grief without make-pretend support is only a grim sort of satisfaction. It can be nowhere as strong as the consolation the believer may derive from thinking that what has happened was God's will. But at least there's nothing illusory about it.

A quote from Woody Allen. It appears at the end of the movie *Love and Death*, which is one of the Woody Allen works that addresses philosophical issues in the most overt manner.

In fact in this part Allen talks straight to the camera. What, he asks himself, has he learned about life? (He has just been executed by a firing squad). That man is divided into mind and body. The mind has access to philosophy, poetry, and all those things, but the body has all the fun. The important thing in life is not to be bitter: it isn't that God doesn't exist, but that he's an underachiever. And don't look on death as the end, but rather as a very effective way of cutting down on expenses.

Although it's of course humorously meant, it's a philosophy of sorts, and many people sleepwalk through life with less.

So much for death. Now: immortality and the afterlife.

If religious belief is gone, lock, stock and barrel, the question whether an afterlife exists is no issue at all. The afterlife is a quintessentially supernatural belief, and thus vanishes if the supernatural is ditched.

If there are no gods there is no heavenly abode, and therefore no place for us—or some wisp of us—to go to. Devils don't exist: there's no hell.

If we consider that a belief in an afterlife is derived from a feeling that it would be too much of a pity to be entirely gone when we have, in Hamlet's phrase, shuffled off this mortal coil, we immediately deduce that this kind of immortality—living on in any kind of spectral sphere—is a vain hope. In two senses of "vain." Vain in the sense that nothing will come of it, and vain because it's based on human vanity.

The magnitude of the vanity can be gauged from the fact that it has traditionally been found better to conceive of an afterlife even at the risk of spending all eternity roasting in hell, than not to live on at all. I.e., one's self is so important that it's better, after one's life has ended, to have one's self forever in the most horrible pain than not to continue having that self.

The life we have, here while we are alive, is what there is. It's quite a lot, considering the alternative, which would be not only nothing before life, and nothing after, but also nothing at all between the two voids, either.

We try to remind ourselves, in the face of our own or others' mortality, to emphasize the time we have managed to live, or the time we've been privileged to have those others with us—rather than the time robbed from us after the advent of death.

Many may see the lack of an afterlife as a pity—"there goes my eternity!" But then, it's also one less thing—a very big thing, with all those eternal punishments—to worry about. There's plenty to worry about right here. Bills to be paid, good actions to be undertaken. Or at least, bad actions to be avoided.

The above paragraphs have constituted an agnostic approach to the question of *human* immortality. As for any alleged immortality of the gods, that's an issue that can only agitate those who believe in them.

Still, it's interesting to note one particular quandary they can get into over immortality. It's because it can refer to two things. Whether gods ever die, or whether they always existed or were at some moment born or otherwise brought into being.

On whether the immortal gods once had a beginning, there is disagreement. This is because of the vexing problem of infinite regress. A god created the world, okay, but who in turn created the god, or the pod (or whatever it was) from which the first god sprang out? And so on, ever further backwards—infinite regress.

This problem naturally only refers to the gods in charge of creation. Other gods can be born to the latter, or spring from their shields or eyelids or something like that, and escape the issue of ultimate origins.

Not so the gods of creation. At least one of them needs to have had an ultimate start. How to deal with the problem of infinite regress? Some people have been willing to settle it by positing eternal existence backwards in time for their gods of creation; some not. Among those who did not, and preferred only gods that were born at some time, nobody seems to have chosen to just *live* with infinite regress in godly births. Instead, they have tended to find it intellectually less abhorrent to decide to stop the regression after a finite number of steps. Usually they have ending the backward sequence with a primeval body of water or an *ur*-egg or similar device. And they have always successfully blocked their minds from asking where that primeval water came from, or who laid that very first egg.

By the way, I don't know of anyone who has applied the mystical-synthesis process to this issue, and conceived of a god who is, mystically, at one and the same time both eternal and created. There's an overlooked opportunity here for religious innovators. I'm giving this idea away for free.

But if godly origins, timewise, are controversial, believers have always been in virtually universal agreement that gods, once they exist, never die (although they may, with the arrival of newer contenders, be neglected and then forgotten).

One exception that many people may point to is Richard Wagner's *Twilight of the Gods*, in which all the gods allegedly die when their abode, the Valhalla, goes up in fire. Nevertheless, even Wagner's main interest, in that *Götterdämmerung*, was to develop a poetical allegory of the collapse of a certain way of being. He didn't seem to devote any clear thinking to what would exist, or not, after the wholesale immolation of the gods at the end of the opera. For starters, although the entire pantheon is supposed to go up in flames, at least some members of that world's extended mythological family—the Rhine maidens—remain alive at the end. So who knows who else happened to be out of town and survived—preparing the way for a possible sequel?

Besides, how do we know for sure that gods can't survive a fire? Even the non-god Siegfried was undeterred by fire in an earlier opera in Wagner's four-part cycle.

Next, the question of reincarnation. For the atheist, given the absence of any belief in an ineffable spirit or essence that lives on after death, there is no reincarnation issue, period.

Reincarnation is a variant of the question of the afterlife, with an interesting twist—many of its believers want to avoid it rather than being pleased with the idea.

Westerners who favor reincarnation tend to think it is a good idea, although they may wish their actual consciousness would travel too, and let them thus be aware of everybody they were before. Only occasionally do they fully gain this awareness.

(Those who do gain memory of their past selves, lend themselves to scoffing by doubters who note that they usually turn out to have been Cleopatra or Charlemagne in the past, and very seldom some nameless serf. But maybe that criticism is unfair— maybe it's precisely because they had such strong personalities in the past that they manage to remember now just who they were. I'm just kidding.)

But then, Westerners are generally individualists, inheritors of a worldview that, with exceptions, has developed and nourished the concept of the individual. The worldview in which reincarnation is seen by its believers as something regrettable, rather than as a fortunate chance to continue living, comes from oriental religions that emphasize the wholeness of the universe at the expense of the individual. Stress is laid on the idea (popular among those who find the diversity of the world distasteful) that the universe is one (or even One, with a capital letter, capital letters meaning that a concept is mystical—save in German, of course). Thus, they see each reincarnation as a postponement of their desired full fusion back into the One.

To expand on some of the above, here's an aside for the more philosophically minded. Maybe it should be underlined that this oneness of the universe is not a physical but a metaphysical position. It says that behind the huge number of seemingly different things, and appearances of things, in the universe, there is only one reality, one kind of ultimate substance. But it isn't an ultimate substance in physical terms, i.e. the simplest element or particle. The ultimate substance is not a substance like others, it's a special, ineffable Substance. And the idea of "one reality" goes beyond having one sole set of physical laws, or anything along those lines, for the entire universe; it is a metaphysical One Reality.

Incidentally, why the usual choice of the number one, instead of some other number? Why doesn't anybody proclaim that the universe has, say, 4 or 39 or 5,807, or even infinite, irreducibly different ultimate realities? It almost goes without saying that this wouldn't emerge from any attempt to go out and actually identify and *count* whatever one has identified as the forms of reality, and then test them for irreducibility to the others. Like the decision that the world is just one, it would invariably be the result of an inner conviction, not of any messy actual research.

To rephrase the question: why the overwhelming importance attached to cosmic unity? Possibly it's a psychological reaction to—a form of protection against—the manifest plurality and complexity of the observable world, which many people find unsettling and abhorrent.

There's no reason why the plurality and complexity of the world should necessarily be regarded as abhorrent. Other people may see the world as more interesting that way. And even if complexity *is* abhorrent, that doesn't prove that reality has therefore, as a favor to us and our preferences, arranged itself in an underlying oneness.

Back to the observed desire, among many believers in a universal oneness, to disappear into it. That means eliminating rather than stressing one's individuality. Self-awareness is seen to be an obstacle to the desired integration with the One. It's the self that stands in the way of bliss. Consequently, if the self, through reincarnation, persists in coming back in other guises instead of fading out at death, separation from the One will go on and on.

From this standpoint, it would have been better if reincarnation hadn't arisen in the first place. However, as repeatedly mentioned, people have historically found it extremely hard to unbelieve things once the belief has got around. It has always been much easier to add levels of new and subtler arguments as a means to wriggle out of philosophical predicaments. They add the provisos and additional assumptions that patch over the problem.

It may be objected that scientists do much the same when they add further hypotheses to maintain a theory that seems to be refuted by an observational fact—rather than immediately discard the theory. Famously, the planet Neptune was discovered because, when Uranus didn't prove to have the trajectory that it should have under Newton's laws of gravitation, those laws weren't discarded—instead, an extra hypothesis was added, namely that some then-unknown planet must be tugging at Uranus. And it happened to be Neptune.

The difference is that, with scientific training, a point is reached when it's agreed that the theoretical structure with all its additional props has become too unwieldy, and it is abandoned for a new one. Religious thought, on the other hand, never ever says, "This is getting absurdly complicated. Let's restart from scratch with different assumptions."

Scientists, by the way, as human beings may personally feel an inner clamor for certainties too. The most famous example was provided by Einstein when he said he couldn't believe that God plays dice with the world. He didn't *like* the increasing element of randomness that was being discovered in physical nature.

However, scientists—at least honest scientists—make a difference between their feelings and actual science. Even if sometimes grudgingly, they eventually cease ruling out their displeasing findings.

A final section before ending this chapter on death and immortality. In no way is this intended to be an "inspirational" book. The aim remains the outlining of solidly lay approaches to life's big questions, no more but also no less. Still, the following ideas do suggest themselves, and for what they're worth, they're included.

There's two parts.

First, I find it helps *me* to some extent—though this kind of consideration is unlikely to console people with a different mindset—to remind myself that in this accident-prone, disease-prone world, packed with people who are either evil or dangerously blundering, or both, the surprising thing is that death isn't even more prevalent.

This standpoint is a byproduct, or application, of a wider-ranging attitude that goes like this: don't expect too much—from anything, including life as a whole—and you won't be so disappointed. And the latter, in turn, may be seen as a consequence of the following piece of advice: don't take yourself too seriously. At least, try not to.

Second part: would you like to live on? There are actually some things you can do.

- Nurture a good memory of yourself among your family and friends. The downside of this is that, unfortunately, it also works if you leave a very *bad* memory of yourself among your family and enemies. However, this is the chapter on death and immortality, not the chapter on ethics.

- Would you like to live on? Donate your organs.

- Put all or at least some of those thoughts, experiences and insights, which you consider a pity to go lost, down on paper. Even if nobody publishes them; even if you write poorly. Who knows who will pick them up and read them some day?

- Do you take photographs? Keep them in some more or less orderly fashion, or at least all together, with the names and dates affixed in some manner. Again, who knows who will take an interest in them when coming across them some day?

- Plant trees.

- Do you do anything with your own hands, like drawing, playing the banjo, making paper dolls, whatever, even if badly? Don't be shy; hand the results out to people, give them recordings of your banjo plucking. Always accompanied by light-hearted rather than solemn words, of course, particularly if you really are pretty bad at these things—but if that's where your heart lies, they may light sparks and live on, and through them, so will you.

- Help the needy, help the community.

- Get involved in undertakings that will live on.

CHAPTER 16
WHAT'S SO SPECIAL ABOUT BEING RATIONAL?

An earlier chapter left dangling the defense of rationalism.

Nothing is perfect in this world (and there is no other world). So it's freely admitted that rationalism is imperfect. Being rational, or leastwise trying to be rational, has its limitations; it needs to be tempered with other virtues, particularly compassion and a sense of proportion in things, including a measure of modesty about one's own rational abilities.

It is also limited in another sense, that of not being the most suitable guideline for the area of life broadly definable as having fun, including one's love life.

And additionally, sometimes an irrational hunch gives better results than our best rational attempts (although we can't be sure that it wasn't actually rational too, only that it operated faster than our plodding mind could follow).

Granting all this, rationalism is still better than the alternative, irrationalism. One strong, in fact conclusive reason is that rationalism allows (in fact, orders) improvement in one's positions. If rationalists conclude that they were mistaken in something, they will seek to correct the mistake—because it's the rational thing to do. Irrationalists have no such inducement within their own system. They may, of course, decide *irrationally* to seek improvement. But then, they may also irrationally decide to make things worse—there's nothing in irrationalism to bar them from it.

From the rational point of view, there's something worse than rationalism's limitations in some areas of human life. It's the thought that the choice of rationalism may itself be suspected of being irrational.

Notice, however, the following: even if that's the case—if the choice of rationalism is itself irrational, with this itself providing one more example of the imperfections of rationalism—that in no way means one should give up on the latter. Since we cannot be *entirely* wise, do we give up trying? If we cannot be as humane and charitable in every act of our lives as we'd ideally love to, is that a reason to give up trying to be humane and charitable? Of course not. Being the best options we have, we do the best we can; we apply them as far as we are able to.

The same with rationalism.

Rationalism—the approach that is guided by logic—can only go so far in some human matters, but it's still the best tool humans have, while requiring tempering with other qualities, like mercy, in those human matters.

In that sense—the sense that rationalism is the best among the available alternatives—the choice of rationalism *is* rational after all. What a surprise.

Believers may believe they perceive a loophole, favorable to their cause of belief, in the above.

If even rationalists admit that rationalism has its limitations in some areas of life, why not fit religion in one of those areas that rationalism is excluded from, or where rationalism is only one guest among others? If that's done, all the arguments in this book at one stroke become utterly irrelevant.

A tempting gambit indeed if you are a believer. But hold your horses.

If we only consider the area of religious belief and practice that is constituted by ceremonies, rituals and all else that makes practitioners *feel good*, by all means go ahead with the gambit, if it gives you harmless pleasure.

But if we consider the area of religion that professes to provide answers to life's Big Questions, which are rational questions— even when they turn out to be based on unexamined false assumptions, or are otherwise wrongly posed, and thus evaporate or need to be rephrased—then, obviously, irrational answers won't do at all. There was no loophole.

The gambit (trying to exclude religion from the demand for rationality) is clearly just another version of religion's plea to be left alone with all those messy logical and empirical arguments, since it admittedly is based on faith alone. That would be fine (for the feel-good factors alone) if religion didn't claim to have answers to rational queries too.

Why didn't I say all this when the issue of rationality first turned up in this book, and be done with it then and there? I just felt that, so early in the book, some readers would be disappointed and turned off by so "meager" a defense—that rationalism, however imperfect as a method and incomplete as an answer to everything in life, is better than the alternatives; it's the best we've got, and thus it's the rational path to choose.

At this stage in the proceedings, if readers are still with me after dealing with mega-issues like death, or the meaning of life, with approaches that essentially don't offer much more consolation than that of being devoid of arbitrary belief, being clear-eyed, and being self-reliant, then they're probably inured and will feel the blow less strongly.

CHAPTER 17
ONE DEITY VERSUS MANY

Should believers opt for one deity, or many? This would seem to only be of importance to believers, albeit of truly colossal importance to them. To outsiders to all systems of faith, whether it's faith in established religions or in simple superstitions—however one draws the line between one and the other—it shouldn't an issue at all. "One or many gods" doesn't make any difference.

And yet, there is one difference, of a *practical* nature, and it's a literally life-and-death practical nature. Polytheism is observably less conducive to violent intolerance than monotheism. In general, polytheism doesn't give its believers an equally strong incentive to get so worked up at the spectacle of others who worship differently that they go out to slaughter them if they don't convert. If they murderously hate other polytheists, or monotheists, it's very often for other reasons, or strongly mixed up with other reasons, e.g. racial, power-based, social or territorial. For one example, it could be because the others have once tried to force their doctrines or practices on *them*.

That about sums it up for the question of one god versus many, except that one may additionally note that "monotheism" is really an ambiguous concept, behind its apparent clear-cut nature.

This is a very sore issue for monotheists. But if one looks at their various systems of belief empirically and without prejudice—like an anthropologist who goes out into the field to study a given people's beliefs—it is seen that it all depends on the *definition* of god that they choose to employ. They may worship other celestial beings, but simply don't define them as gods. By defining them as semi-godly entities, or at least giving them some supernatural status—archangels, angels, humans who behaved in a godly manner, etc.—they see their monotheism as maintained, even when these other beings are also given individual worship.

One may (I don't advise it, because it's such a touchy subject) argue that "real" monotheism ought to utterly exclude the *worship* of anything else than the one god (for instance, the god's mother), or it forfeits that specific status of monotheism; that monotheists are of course entitled to hold any number of other beings in the very highest regard, but as soon as they begin to actually worship them, they cross a line (which their religion itself set up, of course, when it decided for monotheism). Or one may (again, highly touchy!) point out how fuzzy the border is between some of their actual behavior and idolatry, whatever distinctions they claim on the issue.

To which they may retort, with some justification, "Hey, it's *our* religion, and *we'll* define our terms. Who are *you* to tell us otherwise? You don't even believe."

They may add (with less justification, if one has done one's homework about these things), "You just don't understand the difference between our worship of the one god, and our worship of other celestial beings, or between worship of an image and of what the image stands for."

The latter point, even if it were true (and they can't really know what one understands or doesn't) only shifts the question one notch. One might argue that whatever those differences in the nature of the worship, monotheism "should" mean only *one* worship, not several different degrees, or kinds, or levels of worship; and they might counter, again, that *they* decide what monotheism should or shouldn't mean.

Fine. This isn't a federal issue (for us). It *is* an internal matter of theirs. The only point being made—and it's made because non-believers, too, may find it of interest to consider it, just as they may like to follow French politics even if they aren't French—is that it's a matter of the definitions used. Of course monotheists are entitled to make their own definition of what constitutes monotheistic worship. That doesn't make it any less a matter of definition, and they are kidding themselves if they tell themselves it isn't.

CHAPTER 18
WHY BE GOOD IF THERE ARE NO GODS TO ORDER US TO?

This is the (already several times heralded) chapter on ethics.

The question in this chapter's title, or some variation of it, is one of the favorite instruments that believers use as a weapon with which to try to beat atheism. The archetypal variation is, "If there were no religion, no fear of God, what would keep people from stealing and killing?"

This chapter will first counter it in a negative way, then answer it in a positive way, and lastly provide responses point by point.

The first step in a nonbeliever's approach to issues of good and evil is to parry this question by turning the tables on those who raise it. This is easy—ridiculously easy.

Since when, one may ask, has *religion* kept people from stealing and killing? If there's one constant in mankind's history, it's stealing and killing; and throughout history, most people in the world have been believers. From this it necessarily follows that most of the stealing and killing was carried out by believers.

Not only that, but a good share of the killing (often killing of an especially brutal kind) has actually been *triggered* by religious drives.

By rights, believers should be too ashamed to open their mouths at all on these matters. It really takes a lot of nerve for people with such a spectacularly blood-drenched history to lecture others on moral issues of any kind. *They* surely wouldn't take advice from any other group with that blood-curdling kind of history behind it.

As usual, though, they operate on the basis of an idealized image of religion and of themselves. They not unnaturally pay greater heed to that flattering conception—their idea of what things *should* be like—than to the actual historical record.

Nonbelievers are well advised not to take any humbug that religion has now reformed in this sense, either. The last burnings at the stake in Europe took place as recently as the early 1700s (for the record, they were perpetrated in Portugal), a mere blink of the eye in historical terms. And other murders born of religious considerations continue right now. They're in the headlines from around the world, even within the largely secularized West—*vide* the bombings and shootings at abortion clinics in the United States.

Nor is it only a question, nowadays, of individual religious extremists running amuck while all religious headquarters call for nothing but nonviolence and sweet reason. That notion doesn't tally with any officially-issued calls for jihad or death-sentence fatwas. Nor does the idea hold water that these are exclusively Eastern phenomena. A Roman Catholic pope campaigned very hard against the use of condoms amid a worldwide AIDS epidemic; and if such a thing is heeded, it could cause incomparably more deaths than all religion-inspired terrorist bombings, not to mention individual autos-da-fé and stonings of adulteresses, put together.

If the charge is made that all this mistakenly conflates a supposedly pure and goodly religion and the fallible human beings who exercise it, whoever raises the charge can be referred to the crack, in an earlier chapter, that the tree is known by its fruit.

On another front, believers may raise the argument that, even if religion should admit it has a lot to answer for as regards killings perpetrated with religious prompting, religion also has a lot to say about other forms of evil. Believers, for example, can't be accused of stealing or swindling *systematically and for religious reasons.* (For other reasons, of course they *could*, like everybody else).

An answer obviously suggests itself, similar in form to one already used above. Believers themselves wouldn't heed any group that said, "We're not embezzlers or highway robbers, cardsharps or alimony cheats. Our only sins have been torture and murder—so you must listen to us on ethical matters."

This was, essentially, a (much-merited) counterattack—the negative part of a lay approach to issues of good and evil. The part that notes that religion has not solved the problem either and has, in fact, bloodily contributed to it. The positive part follows.

One must note that there are two different underlying assumptions to the question, "what's to keep us from committing evil, without religious restraints?" One assumption, implicit but unmistakable, is that *only* religious restraints can do the trick. The other is that religious restraints *actually do it.*

The second assumption is the one that was demolished above, in the negative part or counterattack. Looking into the first assumption is the positive part of the approach.

Incidentally this chapter, as you may have already noticed, doesn't go into any fine distinctions between "ethics," "morality," "questions of good and evil," "issues of right and wrong," etc. It uses the expressions interchangeably, again merely for variation, because it is interested in treating the whole problem in general terms, and those apply to any and all of these definitions. (This book prefers not to speak of "sin"—because of its built-in religious content—unless it is believers who are being quoted in the way *they* would employ the concept).

The issue of right and wrong involves at least three separate questions: why wrong exists in the world; what is right and what is wrong; and for what reason one should do right (in our case, for what reason one should to right if there's no gods to get us to do it, either by urging us or by scaring us).

Why does evil exist? For believers, or at least for that majority group of believers who put their faith (literally) in hugely powerful celestial beings who are basically beneficial, this is a tremendous problem. It's the same as the problem of the existence of death and pain, and the same analysis applies. For non-believers, it's no question at all. Evil is something that exists in the world that exists, like friendship, or magnetic forces, or, on some people, curly hair.

Still, one can investigate all such things' nature, and also seek, as the case may be, to control, quench, or promote them.

Second question: what is right and what is wrong?

From an atheist standpoint, the first thing to do is to shift aside those kinds of "evil" which are only such within a religious context. For example, the evil of worshipping many gods, in a culture that says there is only one; or the evil intermarriage between members of different social groups (e.g., castes) where religion orders this not to happen. For members of *other* religions, these strictures may be wrong; for non-believers, these things don't come under the heading of "right or wrong" at all, but under that of "irrelevant." A non-believer simply doesn't have to worry whether worshipping a given number of deities is good or evil.

Once everything of that type has been separated, what to do about the rest—how to determine which actions are good and which are evil?

The answer is simple, though aggravatingly imprecise and variable over time and over geography. The aggravation is stronger the more one is accustomed to the clear-cut (well, often so) rules of religion. The answer is: society decides. It is a laborious, ever-continuing process, carried out in the legislatures and in the courts, which are the proper venues for it.

In practice, individuals modify the decisions of the legislatures and the courts within certain limits, as when they choose to ignore a law which they feel to be patently immoral in strictly secular terms, whether religion agrees or not (say, if there's a law to turn in all Jews to a Gestapo), or just stupid (like a law against mispronouncing the name of the state of Arkansas). It's messy, like all human things, but it's the best system we've got. It begs the question of how anything can be considered immoral if it "is" immoral yet a society happens to approve of it—and only society defines what is moral. But the system, by and large, works in practice, despite this circularity, because if enough people feel something is immoral, this eventually finds its way into legislation.

And erecting systems that work in practice, even ones that require frequent tinkering and updating, is the most we can aspire to in the world as it exists.

Religion has no right at all to complain about the way this makes evil a relative, time-dependent and geographically-dependent thing. All it has to do is look back into its own ever-changing past. Let it recall the times when it was seen as morally right (in fact, as ethically most praiseworthy) to murder children. It was called sacrificing them to the gods. Or when it was right and proper for the priest-ruler to marry his sister, or when it was demanded that he sacrifice *himself* if the crops failed or other disasters occurred. Or when it was right to have slaves; or to torture and "if necessary" burn to death those who held different creeds or even different scientific ideas from those of the established religion; or to go to war to turn heathens away from their wrong beliefs, at swordpoint.

The better that religion demonstrates that it has now given such things up as wrong, the more it thereby demonstrates that religious definitions of right and wrong are also relative.

Once again, the decent thing for many religions to do, in view of their past (and some cases, their present) would be to shut up in shame and try to remain inconspicuous in these discussions.

Third question: for what reason should one do right and avoid doing wrong, as socially and/or privately defined? Answer: one does right in order to maintain self-esteem and to gain the esteem of others. One avoids wrong to avoid losing those forms of esteem, and, to put it bluntly, to avoid going to jail.

In other words, under an agnostic's approach to the questions of ethics, in those cases in which personal conscience is insufficient to ensure compliance with social definitions of right and wrong, one has to rely on social containment and action. And here's an arresting point to notice: in practice, this is what *already* largely happens in the secular modern world.

An interesting item to consider is that believers may claim that all, or most, of what we define as agnostic and socially-established concepts of right and wrong, and that we see coalesced in society's laws, have their basis in religious thinking and rules. "You claim it's a secular ethics, but we invented it," they may say.

The answer to this is twofold.

Firstly, to the extent that this is indeed the case (and it largely is), thank you, truly, for the past services rendered—but today we prefer the secular versions, thank you again, for all the reasons, developed over the course of the book, for preferring agnostic lives.

Secondly, if many notions of right and wrong did evolve through religion, it's because society happened to develop with religion as an overwhelming component. If the people with a powerful interest in ethical matters who, at the time, drafted rules of behavior in religious terms, had lived in societies where it was the *lay* authorities who held the power over those matters, they would more likely have shaped them into secular laws, so as to ensure compliance.

"No," it may be countered—"if the framers of the ethical rules were themselves prelates of some kind—as many of them were— they would still have framed them in religious terms." "But," we may then rebut in turn, "in a more secular world it's likely that many of them wouldn't have *become* prelates in the first place." This toing-and-froing can go on quite a while. But in any case, any idea that religion was *essential* to the development of rules of right and wrong will have been thoroughly undermined by the discussion.

Yet another point worth raising is whether one should actively do good, or just avoid doing wrong. Again, a double-barreled approach suggests itself.

The first part is easy. One should try to actively do good, but not be too hard on oneself if all one manages to do is avoid doing evil things. Just avoiding evil is an achievement not to be sneezed at, considering the way much of the world behaves.

The second part is the messy one. It arises from noticing that in practice (and as was only to be expected in our complex world), in all too many cases the choice of avoiding evil isn't so clear-cut. For example, when a legislature issues a law that benefits many people, the measure often has side-effects that harm others. We give an extra hand to groups that are especially disadvantaged, and members of the non-disadvantaged majority press charges of reverse discrimination. And so on.

All we are presented with in most cases, then, is diverse courses of action which all have advantages and disadvantages. We can't absolutely "avoid evil" with any of them.

What to do? What we, in practice, always do: we muddle through, choose what appears to be the least bad among the options available, and try to develop better ones next time.

That necessarily is the real meaning of avoiding evil. Not "never treading on any toes," but "treading on as few toes as possible."

Yet even in this regard one has to watch out not to take this too literally—i.e., it's not exclusively a numerical question, a question of counting the toes trod on, without other considerations. The "tread on as few toes as possible" approach was most clearly enunciated in the utilitarianism of Jeremy Bentham and John Stuart Mill. Utilitarianism is the philosophy that, in simplified form, advocates "doing what will bring happiness to the greatest number of people." If applied blindly, this might lead to the extreme of butchering a minority if a larger number of people, the majority, will benefit from it.

I *said* this part was messy. Still, it's just an example of the usual situation in human affairs. Having to strike such difficult balances, and take so many things into consideration all the time, is nevertheless the best system we've got.

A last issue for this chapter: it may be inquired whether the best course of action isn't clearly marked out (in fact, whether all ethics isn't solved) by the Golden Rule, "Do unto others as you would like others to do unto you"—which one can, after all, take in strictly secular terms. Treat others as you would like others to treat you.

The answer to the inquiry is, alas, no. Of course the Golden Rule is a useful guideline. But it doesn't always clearly indicate the best course of action, nor solve all ethics. Firstly because it ignores the earlier-mentioned, all-too-common cases when there are competing options that help some people in some ways yet harm others, or even the same people but in other ways. In those cases, *which* among the competing groups are the others to whom one should apply the Golden Rule?

Secondly, the Golden Rule seems to have been created on the assumption that everyone is sane and has a positive outlook— which is patently not the case. If you tell pathological masochists, for example, to apply the Golden Rule, they'll badly hurt others because they want others to badly hurt them. No, nobody has managed to develop a simple single rule that covers all cases.

However, the positive points made in this chapter, taken together, are a workable approach to ethical questions while leaving the gods entirely out of it.

CHAPTER 19
IF RELIGION WERE TO DISAPPEAR, WOULD WE LOSE ITS SIDE BENEFITS?

Whatever else one says about religion, it has inspired people to some extraordinary achievements in other fields. Breathtakingly beautiful sacred music, awesome cathedrals, coruscating Islamic architecture come immediately to mind. If everyone abandoned religion in favor of an entirely atheist standpoint in life, would we lose this creativity forever?

No, we wouldn't. The religious impulses that led to the above examples would be gone, but the artistic impulses wouldn't, and they would merely be channeled in lay ways, like grand secular music and grand secular architecture.

Nothing could have kept Bach from composing dazzling, heart-filling and intellect-satisfying music. If he had been born an agnostic in an agnostic world, his output would simply have been music for secular rather than religious purposes. It would certainly be equally dazzling, intellect-satisfying and yes, heart-filling, although people would then normally refer to the latter characteristic using different words—"emotionally-fulfilling," perhaps, rather than "soul-fulfilling."

It may be objected that not everyone is a Bach—an indisputable fact. Others who are talented, but not quite so overwhelmingly bursting with talent, might, in the absence of an extra boost derived from strong religious conviction, be content with lesser pursuits or with lesser achievements in the same pursuits.

That's hard to tell; it's hard to determine how strong an artistic impulse is in itself, since these things are unquantifiable and, in any case, impulses of various types are often jumbled together. But in any case, if we're worried on this account, a lay solution readily suggests itself. Let's *promote* their creativity in lay ways. Let's offer many juicy commissions for the composition of music, many challenging architectural contests, and so forth. Then the artists are certain to come out of the woodwork.

It's not only a question of money, but also of creating opportunity, scope. The great religious buildings of the world—like Europe's splendid cathedrals, the scintillating blue-tiled *madrasas* (Islamic seminaries) of Central Asia, and the wondrous, porcupine-like mud mosques of Africa—were built to fill a need that was felt for such buildings. If we provide a comparable lay rather than religious need, the art will ensue. The construction of grand sports stadiums, which are considered a big contemporary need, and of equally majestic museums and airports, the need for which is indisputable, proves the point.

Music and architecture were used as examples, but clearly this is valid for other fields that religion may point to as evidence of a beneficial influence—like the philanthropic impulse that leads some believers to actively go out and tend to the needy. Believers may prefer to consider that it's the religious impulse that leads some people to become philanthropic. Maybe Mother Teresa would have been motivated to do her work in Calcutta even if she had been lay Ms. Bojaxhiu, though she would have staffed her hospices with people led by lay motivations, not with nuns. Or maybe she wouldn't have—who knows? It's impossible to resolve these counterfactual questions. The factual way it happened was that she was religious.

These are chicken-and-egg dilemmas—which impulse came first, the religious one or the philanthropic one? Or if not, the dilemma will be which was foremost. Rather than waste time trying to solve these conundrums, the rational thing to do is identify what are the things we consider good, like philanthropic work, and work out ways to foster them. Like the Peace Corps, say.

The impulse to devise rules for ethical behavior has already shaded into secular legislative activity, as we have seen.

Creativity, philanthropic impulses, ethics—these are some areas that the disappearance of religion need not affect (except, it's hard to avoid pointing out again, to *improve* ethics by removing one of the most serious excuses some people have for persecuting and killing others). On the other hand, clearly the result of the abandonment of religion wouldn't apply equally to all its attributes.

In an earlier chapter there was a list of many things religion does. It was noted, for example, that religion supplies ruling classes with an instrument of social control. This would naturally vanish. And good riddance.

CHAPTER 20
CAN MIRACLES BE ACCOUNTED FOR?

For religion, miracles are one of its strongest cards. Goethe professed to find proof of God in the "miracle" of Mozart's music. But seriously now, while religion's tenets depend on faith alone, a miracle helps because it is something that's objective, factual, tactile; it's not otherworldly, it's of *this* world. (Well, the cause is otherworldly, by definition, but the effect is of this world). Medical miracles are especially prized exhibits. Many religious doubters have had their doubts erased, or at least vastly mitigated, by a solid miracle.

A sober approach to the issue prevents the secularly-minded from needing to go along that path. And "sober approach" certainly doesn't boil down to simply dismissing all miracles as frauds, hoaxes, collective hysteria or old-wives' tales. It is related, among other things, to the cat tale I will tell shortly.

The credibility of miracles covers a very wide range, like the miracles themselves. Some may indeed be purposeful hoaxes, but it's certainly not necessary to tar them all with that brush. Some others, especially in ancient times, may not have happened at all, or be wildly exaggerated accounts of something that did happen—history provides countless examples of the way people purposefully or unintentionally alter and embellish the things they retell, and the longer ago it happened, the more so.

Possibly the strongest single cause for miracles is people's willingness and indeed need to believe them. People easily work themselves up and convince themselves they have seen things they really haven't: this is verified every day in police and court work, for example. It's just an unfortunate characteristic of the human mind. If what they have witnessed isn't just an accident or a crime, but something they can connect with the religious beliefs they may harbor, there is additionally a psychological drive to distort them in a way that satisfies and ratifies those beliefs.

Yet, again, these are not necessarily the explanations for all miracles. Others that are reported may perfectly well have been things that actually happened. The difference is that they respond to natural causes.

Some of these natural causes we can puzzle out, like the tears of religious statues that turn out to be a manifestation of humidity. Case closed.

But other natural causes we are unable, at least in our current state of knowledge, to discern. In the latter cases, the agnostic approach is to leave the causes labeled "undetermined," unsolved, open, rather than jump to the conclusion that the cause was God. That jump would imply faith in God—at a bare minimum, in his existence—and miracles are presented as something that need not be underpinned by faith but by solid observation. However, even the most solid observation may in some cases not discern the cause—only the event itself.

Seen in this light, miracles turn out to be no different, after all, from the rest of the religious system. Usually, an explanation of a miracle is sought and, since nothing suggests itself that is covered by the current level of knowledge, the jump of faith is made and the event is attributed to the action of a celestial being. Sounds familiar. Instead of a miracle, it might be, for instance, the origin of the universe that's being searched for. The universe is, after all, also an objective, factual, tactile thing.

In this sense, the attribution of miracles to an act of the gods is part of precisely the same pattern, "tell me anything you can't explain and I'll tell you it was the gods who ordered it to be so."

Medical miracles deserve special consideration. The cures at the Roman Catholic shrine at Lourdes in France are the best-known example.

Let's subdivide medical miracles into those that happen to people who are conscious, and those involving people who are unconscious or in a coma. The latter are obviously the most valuable of all from religion's standpoint. (From a human standpoint, of course, they're *all* welcome).

Let's start with the conscious-patient miracles.

Not that we intend to pin everything on this, but the human body is an atrociously complicated thing, and if you read the history of medicine you will realize that the latter only began to be put on a systematic scientific footing in very recent centuries— particularly after the discovery of microbes thanks to the invention of the microscope. There is an awful lot that medicine still doesn't understand, and one of those areas is the precise relation of the workings of the mind to those of the body.

Any doctor may be able to report that some sudden cures, or at least great improvements in patients' health, "just happen." Some are just temporary and their effect vanishes soon after word of a miracle has already spread, but we can exclude these cases from our analysis. Let's look at the hardest cases to explain, the cures that last.

What took place in those patients' mazelike bodies, or in the interrelations between their bodies and their minds, current medicine cannot explain, or they wouldn't say it "just happened." But even not all of these cases are attributed to religious miracles, although for want of a better word, or out of habit, the term "miracle" is often bandied about without really believing the cases have an otherworldly origin. An "unknown natural cause" would be the recommended description.

However, if someone was praying desperately for the person who underwent the unexplained cure or improvement, or if that person has just been blessed by a prelate, or—especially—if he or she had been taken to Lourdes or some comparable locus of miracles, the conviction that it was a genuine religious miracle will be hard indeed to dispel. Few will be found ready to consider the possibility that they were just spontaneous cures like the others that are not accompanied by the religious endeavors—merely contemporary with those endeavors. Most people will see cause and effect.

In some cases, knowing that one is being prayed for, or is being taken to a religious shrine, may indeed be the reason for the cure, or contribute to it, for the mind's power to influence the body is as powerful as is medicine's ignorance of how it happens.

All of this is fairly obvious and well-known.

So now we come to the kernel of the matter, the miracles at Lourdes and similar religious shrines—or through the intercession of someone or something considered holy—that occur to patients who are unconscious or comatose.

In virtually all such cases, the patients can't have "willed" themselves to get better, since they cannot possibly have known they had been taken there. I say "virtually all" and not "all" because in actual fact, among the many things medicine doesn't know is how much people who have passed out or are in a coma really register about their circumstances. Maybe something of what goes on around them does communicate itself to their minds, even if they forget it—or it's too nebulous to describe or for the patients themselves to make sense of—when they awake.

Yet again, we can afford to exclude these questionable cases if they indeed exist. We finally turn to the toughest cases of all, those in which the patients are definitely unaware of everything and can't have helped with their minds. These are the core miracles.

And now I'd like to tell the cat story I promised.

A long time ago I read a story in a magazine—and how I wish I had kept the clipping, to be able to quote the precise source—about the alleged paranormal powers of cats.

Let it be said right away that I am a cat lover, a *strong* cat lover. When I had an old-style, warm computer monitor, there usually was a cat curled atop it as I worked. I just don't believe in paranormal powers, among cats or among anybody or anything else.

Anyway the highlight, the *pièce de résistance* of the article was the story of a cat that lived happily aboard a ship, to such an extent that even when it was in port the cat, which was perfectly free to move about, never went ashore.

One time, as the boat was about to weigh anchor, the cat suddenly dashed madly ashore on the gangplank. Search parties were unable to find it, and the ship left without it. Some time afterwards—you must have guessed it by now—the vessel was caught in a frightful storm, and sank with all hands.

Okay, let's suppose this really happened. And exactly as described (for instance, let's not worry about who told the story in the first place, if the cat's vanishing was a last-minute thing, and all hands drowned thereafter). Let's consider, first, the response to this of someone with a propensity for belief, and then what I would call the sober approach to the incident.

For the former, it's easy. There's only one explanation; the cat, employing powers unknown to science and beyond science's sphere of action, *sensed* that the ship would sink on this voyage, and removed itself expeditiously.

For the mind that *wants* to believe such things (which observationally includes many or even most people, depending on how tightly one defines "such things") that conclusion is inescapable and immediate. It wouldn't be surprising if people with that kind of mind were ready and willing, on the basis of this one incident and of just a small handful of lesser ones, to extrapolate this alleged supernatural capacity to many or all other cats too. It's what the article did.

Even though it was very well informed about cats, the rush to the supernatural conclusion was so categorical that its writer didn't even consider the possibility of attributing the event to the normal cat lover's observation that, well, cats can be very unpredictable and independent creatures. The four-footed hero of this story could simply have had an urge it had never felt before, and poof! it was gone.

The paranormal explanation is incomparably more satisfying, *ergo* it's the one that is adopted.

Still, I certainly wouldn't base all my skepticism on that possibility that the cat simply was experiencing an exceedingly uncharacteristic behavior that day.

Instead, let's essay a scientific approach to the incident.

For that, we need to try to fit this incident into a statistically relevant pattern. Is this the only time this has happened in history, or have there been other such incidents? If so, what was their percentage of the total? In other words, how many times have ships left port with cats aboard, in total, and how many times has a cat behaved as in this case? Not that there's any way that this information can be obtained, but it needs to be, in order to form an educated (as opposed to a wild) opinion—and this is only the beginning of what we need to obtain.

We need to know, for comparison purposes, how many times ships have gone under with cats aboard who had a chance to leave before it happened—*yet didn't*.

And *then* we need to know how many times cats, who had always been aboard of their own volition, have suddenly chosen to rush irretrievably ashore—and the ships did *not* sink.

Only once we have all this information can we even begin to establish if there is a meaningful pattern, and not just a fluke. And even then all we would have, if the pattern is indeed the case, is the fact that the pattern exists—certainly not an account of its cause.

Now we can apply this kind of approach to the core body of miracle cures.

We need to know (at least approximately) how many unconscious or comatose patients have been taken to the shrines. Secondly we need to know how many such patients have *not* experienced any sudden and unexplained cures. Thirdly we need to know how many unconscious or comatose patients—and out of what total number—have had such sudden and unexplained cures *without* having been taken to the shrines.

Only then can we see if the cures are statistically irrelevant, and therefore simply attributable to the spontaneous improvements that happen in medicine, or if enough of a pattern emerges so that we have to begin to suspect that something is really afoot in Lourdes after all.

Since none of this is available, the measured agnostic approach is to leave the issue open—yet one more volume in the vast library of our ignorance.

For what it's worth, an informal impression is that there's nothing statistically significant going on there. Believers are hardly known for a tendency to play alleged miracles down, so if one doesn't hear about more of them, and considering the vast throngs of the ill and infirm that go to the shrines, it seems the cases are indeed few in relation to the total possibilities.

To repeat, this is only an informal impression—the only possible type of impression in view of the paucity of data. It is certainly nowhere near even the always tentative and provisional nature of a scientific tenet—much less the rock-firm conviction of the religious mind that has adopted the opposite position on miracles.

None of this procedural chitchat will impress believers, because for them miracles don't need any pattern at all to be true. God doesn't have to follow any rule, fulfill any quota. *One* isolated miracle is just as much a miracle as any of the miracles in a consistent pattern of them.

However, this reasoning wasn't developed for believers (nor, for that matter, is any reasoning, when they are acting *qua* believers). It was for *non*-believers to use in trying to account for miracles. The conclusion, for the core group of incidents that cannot be attributed to deception, or to observers' willing self-deception, or the unreliability of the relevant historical record, or discernible natural explanations, or natural remissions of disease, and so on, is that there isn't even enough information to determine if there is a significant pattern that needs accounting for. Isolated cases, not falling within a pattern, either fall within one of the above causes (deception, natural remissions, etc.) or need to be left open until we know more, if we ever do.

All the above disquisition on miracles applies equally to premonitions, omens, and comparable phenomena. Typical case: Jane has a dream in which Jack appears very vividly, and later finds out that Jack died in some faraway place at the same time that she had the dream.

If Jane *wants* to believe that Jack's spirit did travel to her in order to appear in her dream, if, in other words, the belief satisfies a strong emotional need for her, nothing will be able to dislodge that belief from her. There is no reason to even try dislodging it (unless for some reason she tries to impose her belief on others by force).

Others, however, should wonder, first, how often other people who Jane cared for died and did *not* appear to her in a dream. And then, conversely, how often she did dream about people and they did *not* die.

People who want to believe will dismiss *all* those other cases as proving nothing at all. On the other hand, they will adopt the one favorable case as proving whatever they want to prove about the existence (and travel possibilities) of the soul, or about out-of-body experiences, extra-sensory perception, or anything else that gives them comfort and reassurance.

For such is the nature of belief.

CHAPTER 21
DO WE NEED LAY ALTERNATIVES TO RELIGIOUS RITUALS?

Some agnostics favor holding secular festivities to replace religious ones. Members get together to carry out mild rituals in the name of lay ideals, not of God; and these gatherings give them the pleasures of participating in ceremonies, for those who enjoy them, and a sense of community, without involving the supernatural in any way.

Are lay ceremonies—say, for a Tolerance Day, for a Separation of Church and State Day, or on the birthday of some late leader of agnosticism—a good idea from an overall perspective?

First and foremost, if there's one thing that a secular approach gives its adherents—unlike religion—it's the freedom to do whatever they want in such regards.

If it pleases people to observe lay rituals, by all means they should go ahead. In fact, if it pleases them *to go back to religion*, by all means they should go ahead. This goes virtually without saying; nevertheless I say it, just to put it formally on record.

It's a matter of choice.

My own personal choice, for what's it's worth to any others who may be interested, is to be skeptical about any ceremonies no matter how secular. I certainly understand the motives that lead some people to them. Not only is it easier to engage in them than to break with religion cold turkey, but apart from the psychological role, ceremonies serve a social function, which can be especially important in a country like the United States where the social component of belonging to a synagogue, church or mosque community is so large.

Still, for me personally there are stronger considerations. I have an overriding mistrust of anything that smacks of mumbo-jumbo; this mistrust is so strong that it carries over into secular ceremonies too. At the deepest level my concern, in this and in everything else, is always with maintaining the maximum possible individual intellectual freedom. My impression is that when one is participating in a ritual (private or collective) of any kind, although it may provide a pleasant feeling if one is so inclined, one has disengaged one's own brain, if only for the duration. The ritual is in charge. And one has become easier to manipulate, too, if the person leading the ritual should ever feel so inclined.

The idea is to think for oneself. But as soon as even this idea is turned into a mantra, the very fact of its being a mantra makes the latter self-defeating. Even people who are ritually repeating "I must think for myself! I must think for myself! I must think for myself!" aren't thinking for themselves.

Plus, of course, most ceremonies and rituals are *not* about the importance of thinking for oneself, and may strike the non-participant as unnecessary hocus-pocus at heart.

The rest of this chapter is only for those secularists who, faced with the free choice of being for or against secular ceremonies, opt against.

It may be argued that nature has hard-wired us to feel a psychological need for ceremony and ritual, much like the argument that it has hard-wired us to crave belief, i.e. hard-wired us to get a kick out of venerating something "higher than us." What is a good secular rejoinder to this?

In the first place, the "fact" that we are hard-wired for all these things is a dubious proposition. We don't know how much is hard-wiring and how much is merely long-standing social habit.

But secondly and more importantly, even if the hard-wiring is real, the decisiveness of hard-wiring has been oversold. Through evolution, nature (itself a word that has to be taken with care—but let's not be sidetracked) has hard-wired us to respond to people who tread on our toes by punching them. Happily, however, we control ourselves. Or should, anyway.

As Katherine Hepburn said to Humphrey Bogart in *The African Queen*: "Nature, Mr. Allnut, is what we are put into this world to rise above."

Except for the theological implications of that bit about being "put" into this world, this says it wonderfully.

As for the other ingredient of the ceremonies, namely the sense of community that it confers on participants, like-minded people can, if they want, have regular meetings (to talk about the pleasures and challenges of life without otherworldly beliefs, for example, or to delve into the lay aspects of their cultural heritage) without the rituals.

Maybe they'll then fear that, without the rituals, they'll lose members fast—that it's the rituals that mainly keep them coming. If that's the case, maybe they can organize *more attractive* events of a non-ritual nature.

CHAPTER 22
DO WE NEED A LAY ALTERNATIVE TO RELIGION'S DIETARY RULES, ETC.?

Religions impose on their followers a diversity of practices like dietary rules, ritual self-mortification (an order to fast at a certain time falls under both categories) and rules of cleanness (like avoidance of certain people, for example menstruating women, if the religion in question happens to consider them "unclean." By the way, this business of holding some people, or some people at some times, to be unclean is one of religion's least appealing features. On menstruation in particular, more below.)

With time these religious practices have tended to become second-nature in their societies. Some have become equated with healthy habits. Individuals who give up these religions, because they personally cease to have otherworldly beliefs, may be torn about the issue of giving up all or some of the practices that are of *this* world.

In some of these practices there may indeed be a component that makes sense strictly from the point of view of healthy living.

The reasonable thing to do is look at each practice as coldly and in a manner as lacking in prejudice as one can muster. Then one can isolate the valuable ingredient, if any, and separate it from the religious trappings. Next one sees if that valuable lay ingredient is already covered by our everyday social habits. Finally, if one concludes it isn't, one can seek to apply it, in a secular form—e.g. not necessarily on the fixed days of the calendar that the religion may order.

Don't be surprised if the final pickings (those that reach that last stage) are slim. In the first place, the cases in which there really was a valuable health or cleanliness point to the strictures may be considerably lower than their proponents maintain—without actually having dedicated more than a few minutes to *thinking* about the issue.

In the second place, where there was a point that indeed survived the hard-headed first examination, the immense likelihood is that it will already have been incorporated, and possibly in a more thorough and scientific form, by the improved medicine and overall habits of cleanliness that have evolved since the days when the point was first glimpsed.

Without denying that a few religious practices (perhaps a handful?) may have incorporated good diet, health, cleanliness or similar points, one reason to examine them with special skepticism is that they arose in the same periods, and very likely from the same impulses, that led to such phenomena—typical of anatomically and physiologically ignorant early societies—as an obsession with menstruation, which is quite a widespread characteristic of old-established religions. Fear of, and revulsion at, what isn't understood is a constant in human society—although in the specific case of menstruation, and the ensuing taboos related to its "unclean" nature, an added element of misogyny is hardly to be ruled out.

An obsession with sex (I'm talking now of sex in general, not just its manifestation in menstruation) is normal human nature; if sex is so much fun, why shouldn't it be? What is not normal is *fear* of sex (again, in general, not the specific fear of catching a disease through it). Rules of self-mortification involving sex—like celibacy—are to a great extent an expression of such fear, whatever superstructure of belief are added to it, like the idea that celibacy helps the celibate to concentrate better on the Absolute or something along those lines.

But it's all jumbled together—fear and mistrust of sex and an obsession with it as something dangerous and bad, especially when its workings aren't fully understood, and always because it leads people away from docile obedience to strictures.

Therefore, one has every right to be very suspicious of rules that originally were, or still are, somehow linked to sexual matters in general.

Still, despite all the above, maybe a religion-derived rule for a healthy habit is found that escapes those caveats. Imagine it's found that a certain religion orders that hands always be washed before handling food. (Simply that—not, for example, "wash your hands before you handle food if your hands have previously touched an object used by a member of a lower-class group of people, or have touched a woman with her period, or seven days before her period, or seven days after it.") What then? Simple. We thank that religion for having developed that rule, and *we* follow the rule not because the religion says so, but because we know about the existence of germs that transmit disease and that can be eliminated with soap and water.

In other words: we should wash on all those occasions (like handling food) when, now that we understand the process, we know we need to in order to prevent illness, infection and odor; and not, blindly, on occasions merely dictated by ancient ritual yet unrelated to, or misunderstanding, those occasions. For instance: should a religion indicate washing before sitting down to a meal, and then, before actually eating, order that some sacred object be touched that has not itself been washed, then the washing has been defeated, and it would show that it didn't really understand its own beneficial idea.

Anyway, there actually aren't that many such beneficial religious rules that do have an empirical scientific footing. The vast majority of things that have indeed improved our health and lengthened the average lifespan have been derived from empirical science, not religion. If people say otherwise, their counter-examples usually boil down to just one or two, maybe three.

Special mention is merited by ritual mutilations—cutting off, or slashing away at, parts of the body on religious grounds. E.g., circumcision, male and female, or the scalp gashing some Muslims practice, on themselves and on their children, on the day of Ashura; stand by for a practical suggestion in this regard.

Ritual mutilations are virtually a definition of barbaric custom. (Barbaric in both customary senses: brutal and primitive). Even the alleged health benefits of male circumcision—the supposed health gains, which in a few countries, like the U.S., caused it to be adopted as a secular habit too—are nowadays discredited: the ultimate health benefit that the practice may once have brought can be obtained just by washing the penis regularly. The claimed exception that is AIDS-related will be turned to in a minute.

The fact that the benefits have been discredited is not as widely known as it should. Still, when circumcisions are a profitable little sideline in surgery, maybe it's unsurprising that doctors don't expend too much effort in spreading the news.

One shouldn't, perhaps, be too tough on people, and not just religious people, who still cling, without examination, to such notions as that the body is better off with some part sliced off—considering the claptrap that was believed about the appendix, for instance, only a few decades ago, when appendices were routinely extirpated in principle, not if and when they were infected.

Then there is the equally recent "self-evident" belief that babies needed to be regularly purged (some research has even suggested that what this did to the intestinal flora may not have been unrelated to the prevalence of appendicitis in those days).

But the fact that medical beliefs can also be cockeyed does not justify grotesque, cruel and/or barbaric religious—or just religion-derived—practices. Medicine is a science in progress, and by and large improves over time. Religion is set in marble and in granite, and although it does evolve too, despite the strenuous efforts of most of its leaders, this evolution is incomparably slower.

Enough is enough. And the gorier any religious practice that calls for bloodletting, the more so. But here's the practical suggestion I promised: a symbolic stand-in could be used. There are lots of precedents for this. A special loaf of bread, for example, could have its tip sliced off, or, for Ashura, be slashed, as a substitute. The religious intention would be fully preserved if preserving it is what the practitioners want to do. And any god involved would be equally pleased.

About AIDS: there have been medical reports that found, in essence, that circumcised males were less likely to catch it. I would say this: let's not be hasty with regard to initial medical studies on *anything*. We are all too familiar with the situation in which one study finds something, and later another study finds the opposite and says it's because the original study failed to take this, that or the other into consideration. If what a medical study recommends is something innocuous like, say, eating either fewer olives or more of them, then fine, one can jump to obey if one feels like it. But those studies that by inference advocate measures that are drastic and irreversible, like cutting off parts of the body, should be treated far more cautiously. In this particular example, there is the eminently sensible option of using condoms.

CHAPTER 23
FREEDOM

Are we really free agents?

In one sense, the very question is a laugh. Am I free? There seem to be nothing *but* constraints all around me, and inside me too. I can't get more done by cutting down on sleep, because of biological constraints—I *need* the sleep. I can't take that bauble I see there that belongs to somebody else, because of both legal and psychological constraints—I'll get arrested, and suffer pangs of conscience too. I can't leave this glass standing here in the air because of natural constraints—gravity will cause it to come crashing down. I can't wear that loud jacket I love to the opera, because of social constraints. I can't quit my job and spend my time travelling around the world, because I don't have enough money—not that the amount of money in the pocket is the only economic constraint on people's lives. Anyway, even if I did have the money, I couldn't visit country A because of political constraints, or country B because of military constraints.

And I can't get *too* friendly with that attractive lady over there, because my wife has eyes on the back of her head, and there'll be hell to pay. (A secular hell, of course).

If we've heard about the territorial habits of birds, we may feel sorry for them—in theory they enjoy the freedom to fly anywhere they please in the world, yet in practice they remain bound within strict territorial limits. And then we reflect that we supposedly smarter, more evolved creatures, even those who habitually travel all over the world, far from doing whatever we want, whenever we please, are forever bound in even more ways than birds are.

But that, of course, isn't the only sense of "freedom."

The sense of freedom that's of central interest to this book's subject matter doesn't refer to freedom from the kind of constraints mentioned above. Much less to freedom from political tyranny or colonial occupation, say. Nor does it refer to the idea that we are totally bound by our physical and chemical natures, i.e. by the past of the particles that form us (an idea that seems to be held even by scientists who admit how little we know about what makes life life, and what consciousness ultimately is and therefore how much it controls and how—though much more can be said about this. You can also refer back to the paragraph, in chapter 5, on Leibnitz and whether I move my hand freely either to the right or to the left).

What our present query centers on is freedom as opposed to our acts being determined by fate, the gods, or anything else along those lines.

If the potential competitor against our freedom is a god, a panoply of gods or any other celestial being or beings, then from the non-believer's standpoint there is, by definition, no argument. If there's nothing "out there," obviously our actions are free from any control by that nothingness. There's naught more to do or say on this, except to flash the "The end" sign for the discussion.

Ah, but there could be a sequel. How about our actions being controlled by a disembodied destiny?

Again, no. To believe in an abstract fate—a fate not dictated by gods—or something else of that type is just as untenable, or as solely based on a faith which one is under no obligation to share, as believing in the gods themselves. It is open to the same arguments.

In sum, yes, in this sense we are free.

About how to behave within this freedom, and why "behave" at all, refer back to the chapter on ethics.

CHAPTER 24
ABORTION, CONTRACEPTION, AND SUICIDE

A secular approach to life can have no ethical problem with contraception. All that remains is to await the day when science has progressed to the point where contraception is safer and easier than now. A technical matter, that's all.

Abortion is a trickier matter. The day may come when contraception has progressed to the point that abortion is virtually never even contemplated (except on medical grounds, when, again, there is nothing to argue about), simply because the only pregnancies will be wanted ones, unless they are the result of rape. In that sense, abortion too should be a technical matter. However, we live in the here and now, where contraception hasn't reached that ideal stage, and we have to make decisions now.

Obviously, agnostics won't be guided by the argument that the life of the fetus belongs to God, or anything along those lines. But it *is* life, albeit still an inchoate one, at the very least in the sense that every living cell is, by definition, life. From a reasonable agnostic standpoint, the life of someone who is actually fully living, like the mother, has a higher priority. Other than that general guideline, there is little in the fact of being a nonbeliever that necessarily influences the decision one way or another. Agnostics tend to place a high value on freedom of choice in everything, so that the general trend is to favor the right to abortions. But with abortions posing such complex issues, there is no reason for an atheist not to oppose them. Automatic espousal of abortion rights is not to be assumed.

The best help a secular approach can give is to encourage everyone to evaluate each situation, each case, dispassionately, on its merits, rather than blindly on the basis of a received opinion (which is not to "evaluate" it at all). This actually applies to everything, of course.

Abortion is an issue that falls under the same overall considerations about what is wrong and what is right that were seen in the chapter on ethics. In other words, it falls to the usual interplay between opposing needs, individual consciences, the legislatures, and the courts. Which isn't bad.

The same for suicide, with the usual observation that, as far as the law is concerned (where it is illegal to attempt it), this is an atypical crime because the successful criminal cannot possibly be prosecuted. Whether it ought to be decriminalized, or, further, whether medically-assisted suicide should be allowed, is a matter for evolving law to decide in each society. From the point of view of nonbeliever's consciences, their lives indubitably belong to nobody else than to themselves and, crucially, their families. End of story, except for two very powerful observations.

First, even for people who for some reason or another want death—for any other than truly unbearable and irreversible medical reasons or the like—there is no need to rush into it, because they're sure to get their wish eventually anyway. Since at some point they'll get as much death as they want, they might as well hang around in the meantime, for the satisfactions that come with life, however paltry they may be in some individual cases. They can be anything that pleases or has once pleased them and just might please them again, even just the pleasure, say, of biting into a slice of pizza. There is, alas, no pizza after death.

The other strong observation is that even just a few good moments are worth a lifetime of tribulations.

It may be objected that telling potentially suicidal persons there's no need to rush it, they'll die anyway—and then will have all the death they want, but forever—won't be of much help to desperate individuals with, for instance, a catastrophically low sense of self. Maybe so. But notice that the people who try to help them do raise a lot of other considerations that may not do the trick either. So, if they're going to give them advice after everything else possible has to be done to dissuade them, why not give them this one too, which is a consideration they may not even have thought of?

Then, on a practical note, they might tell them to go and assist people who are in some way even needier than they are; for instance, if they're blind, they could be of service, even if it's only by providing company, to people who are blind *and* quadriplegic. Being helpful to others seems to be, psychologically, most helpful of all to themselves.

CHAPTER 25
SALVATION, GUILT, EVOLUTION, RITUALS

Salvation: this concept only has sense within a system that posits the existence of the soul. Nonbelievers—soulless creatures each and every one—are of this world and only of this world. It is here and now that they must live with their conscience. This is an ethical question, which has already been dealt with. As for their future legacy, that likewise is an issue already discussed earlier.

Guilt: a resource much valued by Roman Catholic priests and by Jewish mothers. (There's also the sense of guilt not for something done by oneself but as something inherited from one's forefathers eons ago—an idea dismissed not only by agnostics but by believers in religions outside the Christian mold). Once more it's a question related to one's conscience, and so it's back to ethics yet again.

Evolution: if the question is evolution versus creationism, this issue is beneath discussion.

However, there is also a different matter that involves evolution, and this one does deserve mention. There are those who hold that religiosity is an evolutionary adaptation. It may perhaps be described in terms like these: in primitive societies, having religious beliefs led to the carrying out of communal rituals, the rituals in turn fostered social cohesion, and social cohesion aided group survival. Thus, religion has an evolutionary component.

If so, what to do? First, to once more remember the business of people stepping on one's toes: the evolutionary response may be a punch, but civilization has (hopefully) intervened to prevent it. Rules of civilized social interactions are also an evolutionary adaptation; and likewise using our brains to decide on things. So, second, we find we have no need to behave in any given manner (in the present case, abide by religion) simply because it was favorable for our ancestors in the Bronze Age, the Stone Age, or even earlier.

Rituals: just as nonbelievers should hold that others must be free to believe whatever they want—with the only proviso that *they* be allowed not to believe anything—they should also hold that believers must be free to express their beliefs through any rituals they like, short of seriously bothering others. I say "seriously" because some expressions of belief involve, for example, making very loud sounds, but that is generally not serious; many nonbelievers necessarily caught within earshot actually *enjoy* hearing muezzins calling, gongs resounding, ram horns blaring or church bells tolling. However, all this said, there is one thing that nonbelievers usually tend to prefer, and fortunately so: that the rituals not involve bloodshed, please. Animal or human.

CHAPTER 26
INSULTS

Apart from the right not to believe—which is part of the demand that religious people should keep from forcing their views on others, which they've historically found so imperative—there's another thing atheists have a right to demand. No insults, please.

Even in this day and age, and in societies where ecumenism is prized and prelates bend over backwards to say nice things about other religions—or at least avoid saying nasty things about them—many of them still consider themselves free to use "atheist" or its logical synonym, "godless," as an insult. Believers outside the hierarchy do this too. This should stop. Nonbelievers don't use "religious" as an insult, but as a description; the religious-minded should please reciprocate. Arguments, if they will, by all means; but no vituperation.

One can easily understand why atheism is the last frontier of ecumenism.

My mother grew up Jewish in a small town where there was no Jewish high school, and my grandparents sent her to a Catholic school instead. The nuns made no effort to convert her; on the contrary, when it was time for her to take the Hebrew lessons and other Jewish instruction she got on the outside, they would remind her and see that she was promptly on her way.

If she couldn't be a devout Christian, they wanted her at least to be a devout Jew. These were only nice, simple, quasi-rural nuns, but they clearly glimpsed the essence of the matter. The quarrels within and among religions are fanatically bitter, but each religion's real, bottom-line enemy isn't another religion but no religion at all. God forbid—never was the expression used more advisedly—that people should give up believing in any religion. Each religious establishment must feel that if that ever happens, there goes its entire *raison d'être*, not to mention its livelihood. If ever there was a clear-cut vested interest, religion's interest in keeping people believing is it.

That self-interest is what makes it so hard for it to stop insulting nonbelief, not the slighting of its gods by not believing in them, or any actual misdeeds by nonbelievers.

It should be stressed that holding that atheists aren't good enough to hold high public office—with the obvious implication that their morals are deficient—is one such insult too. A very serious one. Not to mention stupid and one that believers should be ashamed of, considering the moral deficiencies exhibited by so many rulers who have been religiously minded or even devout.

CHAPTER 27

BEYOND EVERY LAST GOD—COPING WITH ANY CLINGING SUPERSTITIONS

You may face one last problem. You may affirm in all truthfulness that you don't believe in any gods or in otherworldly interventions of any kind, but still discover that you adhere to other, minor, beliefs or practices that *you yourself* consider to be mere superstition.

This book's advice is: don't get too worked up over it.

This isn't mere self-indulgence. There is a justification for adopting this forgiving attitude. This last chapter shows what the justification is.

First, a little reminder, just in case it's necessary, that one man's superstition is another man's august belief, and vice versa; the boundary between religion and superstition is therefore vague (someone *could* build an entire religion, with priests, otherworldly rewards and punishments, and everything else, even schisms, around the colors of cats or the hanging up of horseshoes in the proper position for good luck). The boundary that really matters to nonbelievers is the one that brings together all conceptions based solely on faith or diverse feel-good factors.

Two arguments sometimes arise with regard to superstitions, however defined.

The first one, argument 1, goes something like this: "the rest of the things you enumerate are indeed superstitions—but not (say) palmistry. *That* provenly works! A palm-reader told my sister that X would happen, and X happened."

Palm-readers (and astrologers, soothsayers and so on) make a fine art of saying ambiguous things, things that can be construed in several ways, to make it easy for the willingly gullible to fit whatever does happen into their predictions. Also, with regard to those occasions when they do appear to hit a legitimate bull's-eye, it's necessary to see (as with miracles) what percentage of total cases that represents. The palm-reader may also have predicted Y, which didn't happen, while Z did happen and the palm-reader didn't predict *that*; but the believer only pays attention to the hits.

The main thing is that if people wield the argument that one particular superstition actually works, on the basis of its having scored a few hits here and there, they basically betray a *will* to believe it, and this, in effect, restarts the whole book from scratch. Go ahead. I have no objection to the book being reread by the superstitious, of course, but I do recommend that a second copy of it be bought for this purpose. Doing it that way brings good luck.

Argument 2 takes roughly this form: "don't dismiss (say) telepathy so readily, because it may be merely an as yet unknown or undemonstrated force or energy or effect at work."

In answer to that: hey, it's not nonbelievers who think they know all the answers—it's believers who do that. *Of course* nonbelievers admit that new discoveries may alter today's knowledge. Round-earthism may once have been considered a superstition. But nonbelievers (by definition) ask to be allowed to be skeptical of things grounded only on the will to believe them until, and if, proven otherwise. The difference with believers, in this sense, is precisely this willingness to allow themselves to be proven wrong. Circularity again: argument 2 also remits them back to the book as a whole.

This time around it's best to pay for a third copy of the book. That's even luckier.

To press on with the aim of this last chapter, look at the following seven statements:

Stepping on the cracks between the flagstones of the sidewalk will bring bad luck.

Some people have the power of the evil eye.

The potion in this jar turns people invisible.

When Jupiter enters the constellation of Leo it's auspicious for people of that sign and also for those of other signs associated with fire, like Aries.

The sacrificial dismemberment of Purusha, the primeval man, mind or consciousness, gave rise—as described in the *Rig Veda*—to the four castes, the world, and more. From his mouth came the Brahmins; from his arms, the warriors; from his thighs, the common people; from his feet, the Sudra or menials; from his head, the sky; from his mind, the moon; from his eye, the sun; from his feet (again), the earth.

Through transubstantiation, i.e. a change in the actual substance of the Eucharist, as determined by the Council of Trent, Christ becomes literally present in the wafer that communicants then swallow during holy communion.

When travelling over this mountainous road, it's advisable to propitiate the spirit of the mountain with an offering.

There is no truly essential difference among the seven, however indignantly the differences may be presented by some of the respective believers.

In fact, that very indignation points to what constitutes the main *real* distinction that can be made among those various statements. Some have the proven ability to make many people quite ready to kill others because of disagreements over them. On the other hand, there is no record of inquisitions, crusades or jihads over such issues as the inadvisability of stepping on the cracks between flagstones.

Given the blood-drenched history of religion, one should never dismiss the importance of this difference that exists among these beliefs in their practical effect. But that doesn't mean there's a real difference among them *qua* beliefs. Take a given religion, and not only an atheist but also a member of *another* religion may consider that it essentially is a superstition that has simply been around long enough to become fully systematized and widespread.

This book, it will have become very clear by now, certainly takes an identical attitude to them all and to everything supernatural in between.

All this said, we can deal with the final "practical" problem.

There are those people who are otherwise truly lay-minded in their approach to the world but discover, to their chagrin, that they cannot shake off some residual superstitions.

They really don't believe in any gods or even in any other celestial entities of lesser rank, like saints, angels, demons or evil spirits. Nor do these nonbelievers engage in any religious observances whatsoever, be they ever so slight.

These thoroughgoing atheists, in sum, assign the same verisimilitude to *Genesis*, to voodoo and to *Hansel and Gretel*.

And yet...and yet...even if they wouldn't confess it openly, in their heart of hearts they know they still subscribe to some minor irrational beliefs (like thinking that 9, say, is their lucky number). They wish they didn't—but the superstitions won't go away.

What to do? Suppose you are one such person, and that to your own vexation, because you're absolutely positive it's nothing but nonsense, you hate it when you're thirteen at a table. You don't actually make a fuss—but you can't get over a certain unease.

Or you always put on your right shoe before the left, not just out of habit but for luck—and feel silly, but don't want to risk stopping the ritual.

Or you have heard it said that wearing a red ribbon around the wrist will keep not only hexes and spells away, but also arthritis, and you know full well that there's no conceivable mechanism by which this can possibly work even under the most flexible definition of "non-traditional medicine." But for a while you put one on your wrist anyway, "just in case." "It can't do any harm."

Or you're on an airplane and don't want to even think about engine failure out of a fear, which you know perfectly well is absurdly irrational, that your mere thinking about it could, in some unknowable way, cause it to happen.

If you are one such person, you may find that the worst part of it isn't living with that fear of bad luck or whatever—it's the contempt at your own weakness. Should that indeed be the case, it's because you have noticed, or at least intuitively suspected, an unwelcome corollary to the position that all non-rational beliefs are essentially indistinguishable *in their nature*, i.e., as non-rational.

The corollary is that, things being so, believing in the mildest little superstition is "just as bad" as going along, kit and caboodle, with a whole complex religion featuring a heavenly host of thousands, millions of followers, elaborate rituals and an entrenched clergy.

However, let's look at that phrase, "just as bad," because it can mean at least three different things.

Firstly, it can mean that the two practices—the trivial little superstition and the colossal structure of irrational assumptions and conclusions, fairy tales and perfumed ceremonies—are the same from an intellectual viewpoint. In this first sense, yes, they are the same; as regards applying the intellect, size—the size of the irrational belief—indeed doesn't matter. And this point is not to be minimized.

The phrase "just as bad" can also mean, secondly, that the two are the same from the viewpoint of an exercise of the will. In this sense, no, they are not the same: they are totally dissimilar, because the believer wants to believe, finds warmth and happiness and consolation in doing so—and you are fighting it.

Or the phrase can mean, thirdly, that the two are "just as bad" in their practical effects. In this sense they are again different— utterly so. Earlier in the book it was argued that religion isn't just false, it is dangerous. Three distinct dangers were listed. Assuming that your clinging superstition isn't belief in a prophecy that induces you to slaughter a whole generation's first-born—or something else along such drastic lines—then the answer is definitely no. Your tiny superstition is nowhere near "as bad" as religion in the crucial sense of its practical effects.

So don't be too hard on yourself. In two senses out of three, your little superstition is *not* as bad as believing in a complete system of religion. And two out of three ain't bad.

Instead, gradually free yourself from the remaining mental barnacles, if you can, but without fretting too much over it.

You're already on the right track; and, although it would be nice to achieve it, it isn't so absolutely essential to expunge every last iota of irrational belief or practice.

Why? Because demanding that this be done would be agnostic fundamentalism. And we can leave fundamentalist impulses to the religious.

Nicholas E. Meyer, a globetrotter in special thrall to exotic destinations like Samarkand and the Amazon, the Antarctic and the Gobi Desert, has found that being on the road has proven particularly favorable to philosophical thinking. In a lifetime of probing the issue of religiosity and how to live without it, he has never passed up an opportunity to hone his arguments in debate with people he has met along the world's pathways—the arguments that have now been distilled into this book. Meyer hails from Argentina like another person much concerned with religion: the pope, Francis (Their attitudes in this arena being, of course, quite radically different). A writer, likewise, of other non-fiction books plus one novel, Meyer has been a bilingual United Nations information officer at UN headquarters in New York as well as having engaged in multiple other journalistic and related activities, such as editor, lecturer, screenwriter, travel writer, foreign correspondent, book reviewer, movie critic, cartoonist, and humor columnist. The latter may account for his occasional peppering of the book with caustic little remarks on human nature in general.

www.ingramcontent.com/pod-product-compliance
Lightning Source LLC
Chambersburg PA
CBHW030105070426
42448CB00037B/974